Complete Starter Guide to
Making Bread

From Buns to Baguettes
Essential Recipes for All Bakers

Portions of *Complete Starter Guide to Making Bread* (2024) are taken from *Self-Sufficiency: Breadmaking* (2016), published by IMM Lifestyle Books, an imprint of Fox Chapel Publishing Company, Inc.

Portions of *Complete Starter Guide to Making Bread* (2024) are taken from *Amish Community Cookbook* (2017), published by Fox Chapel Publishing Company, Inc.

ISBN 978-1-5048-0144-7

Library of Congress Control Number: 2024940861

To learn more about the other great books from Fox Chapel Publishing, or to find a retailer near you, call toll-free 800-457-9112, send mail to 903 Square Street, Mount Joy, PA 17552, or visit us at *www.FoxChapelPublishing.com*.

We are always looking for talented authors. To submit an idea, please send a brief inquiry to acquisitions@foxchapelpublishing.com.

Printed in China
First printing

Complete Starter Guide to
Making Bread

From Buns to Baguettes
Essential Recipes for All Bakers

Kathryn Hawkins

Read. Learn. Do What You Love.

18 **38** **46** **84**

Contents

93   111   147   156

Many of us enjoy bread on a daily basis. If you've ever thought about making your own but think it's too challenging, the process requires only a basic level of culinary skill, and the reward is well worth the effort.

Introduction

Making bread is truly fascinating. A food that contains a few very simple ingredients—flour, water, yeast, and salt—when given the correct conditions and care, work together to make something that most of us eat and enjoy every single day. Bread is one of life's simple pleasures. Nothing beats a slice of freshly baked bread and butter or a freshly ripped crusty chunk dipped in olive oil.

The process of making bread dough can be regarded as therapeutic—there's nothing better for relieving a bit of tension than thumping and kneading dough on a kitchen tabletop! Adapting a recipe by adding extra ingredients and shaping the dough to fit your requirements is creative. Filling your kitchen with the delicious smells of a fresh bake heightens the senses. And, of course, the finished product tastes great and is guaranteed to bring satisfaction. Bread is the staple food of many diets all over the world, and being able to make your own means you can provide tasty and nutritious loaves for yourself, your family, and your guests.

This book aims to provide anyone who wants to make their own bread a good grounding in all the essentials that go together to make the perfect loaf. You'll find a guide through the ingredients, as well as a simple explanation of their role in making dough. This is followed by an in-depth look at the different stages involved in breadmaking. It might look a bit daunting at first glance, but it really is very straightforward once you get going. Just a few simple guidelines and you'll be well on your way to creating your perfect loaf.

Once you've read through the basics, you'll find the all-important recipe section. These pages should provide you with instructions for all the basic loaves you might want to cook, from a simple white loaf to more luxurious enriched breads. There are recipes for gluten-free baking as well as yeast-free loaves, and throughout this section, you'll find hints and tips for making variations in flavor, texture, and shape. All recipes are or can be adapted to be vegan-friendly.

You don't need any fancy equipment. Once you've got your ingredients organized, you should be able to get started right away. Soon, you'll be enjoying the tempting aroma of your own loaves baking in the oven and the taste of delicious, healthy, freshly made bread. Happy baking!

An excellent loaf, like this Free-Form White Loaf, can be made with four basic ingredients: flour, yeast, water, and salt.

In many cultures, bread plays a significant role and is often part of family traditions. Here, a family shares bread during Ramadan.

A Brief History of Bread and Making Bread

Bread is a familiar food recognized all over the world. It is sometimes referred to as "the staff of life" and provides vital sustenance from times of famine and hardship, when individuals often survive only on bread and water. It is also found in feasts and festivals when bread is an integral part of a celebratory meal.

Bread has been a mainstay in culinary and cultural life since prehistoric times. It has been the center of religious customs and superstitions for centuries. For example, in some Christian traditions, the "breaking of bread" during the Holy Communion symbolizes the body of Christ; crosses on fruity spiced bread buns at Easter represent the crucifixion; loaves hung in houses on Good Friday ward off evil spirits; and loaves baked with a cross cut into the tops is a ritual to "let the Devil out."

Baking bread during the Christmas season often served as a symbol of hope for good crops as well as good fortune for families in the upcoming new year. Sourdough bread is one of the popular types of bread to make during the holiday season.

Other breads are baked for specific occasions: hot cross buns for Easter, matzo for Passover, and abundantly decorated loaves for Harvest Festival to signify fertility and abundance for the year ahead. The *pan de muerto* is made for Mexico's Day of the Dead and is bread decorated with bread bones to symbolize the cycle of life from birth to death. After the breaking of the fast at Ramadan, iftar, bread is an important part of the meal that follows, representing sustenance and nourishment.

Before specific tools were invented, flour was made by grinding and pounding grains and seeds, stone on stone.

With the invention of tools like as pestles and mortars, people were able to grind grains and seeds more easily and consistently.

The evolution of bread goes hand in hand with developments in crop raising, milling, and baking. Grain production is completely reliant on climate. In Europe, West Asia, and the Near East, thrive the grains that give bread its chewy texture, such as wheat, rye, and barley. Where the climate is less suitable, such as East Asia, other crops like rice have become the staple of choice.

Since humans started using tools two to three million years ago, they were able to grind grains and seeds to make a coarse flour by using a pestle-and-mortar-type utensil. These simple flours were mixed with water and cooked in the fire or on hot stones to make hard, flat breads. This "bread" was a common part of the diet in late Stone Age life in parts of the world where grain grew well. Today, this basic technique is still used in recipes like roti, chapati, and tortillas—all forms of this ancient cooking method.

As civilizations and machineries developed, this simplistic grinding process was superseded by two flat stones, referred to as "saddle stones," pressing

Tortillas are still made as they were in the Stone Age by mixing the flours in water and cooking it over a fire, such as over a stovetop, to create a flat bread.

Saddle stones were created in ancient civilizations to obtain a finer grain dust that was more ideal for breadmaking.

against each other to produce a finer grain dust. This method is represented in Egyptian hieroglyphs, and the stones themselves have been excavated in many parts of the world.

The ancient Egyptians are credited with leavening bread, although they probably discovered the process by accident. No doubt a batch of simple dough was left out in the open and became contaminated with wild yeasts in the air. In the warmth of the sun, the dough began to ferment and rise. When these newly created "yeasted" breads were baked, they were lighter in texture and were easier to eat than the usual flat baked loaves.

Alongside this baking creativity, Egyptians were wine and beer makers, so they knew how to use yeast in these processes. It was only a matter of time before they put the two processes together. Soon, the bakers discovered that a piece of this fermented dough could be added to a fresh batch of dough to make it rise. By 2,000 BCE, bread had become so popular in Egypt that there is evidence of a professional baking industry, producing leavened and traditional flat breads.

When the Israelites fled Egypt, they left behind the leavened bread they had been

Due to the popularity of bread in Ancient Egypt, Egyptians began commercially producing leavened and traditional flat breads, which was confirmed by Egyptian hieroglyphs.

used to. After praying for food when they found themselves starving in the desert, their prayers were answered when they discovered tiny, sweet-tasting grains (probably lichens blown in on the desert wind). They were able to grind this plant material to make porridge and their own flat breads. And so, the origin of Passover unleavened bread, matzo, became a tradition.

Wheat wasn't grown in Greece and the North Mediterranean until around 400 BCE. Until then, bread made from barley was the mainstay. Once wheat was embraced as part

Koulouri Thessalonikis, Greek sesame bread rings, date back to the Byzantine Empire. Today, they are a common street food in Greece.

of the diet, the people from this region began making dough from partly refined wheat flour and whole grains. Soon they regarded these "white" loaves as superior and fit for the gods. They also added seeds, honey, fruit, and nuts to doughs and enriched their loaves with olive oil.

The spread of the Roman Empire saw the real development of breadmaking. The less-reliable, spontaneous fermentation processes of the Egyptians were phased out and replaced by a reliance on brewers' yeast, a technique picked up from the Gauls, who added beer to their doughs. Bread in its many shapes and forms became a central feature in late-Roman culinary life, and a vast amount of wheat was imported from North Africa and beyond to keep up with the popularity. The Romans used teams of animals or enslaved people to operate massive geared grinding stones that produced flour on a much larger scale, and they also used sieves to remove the coarse outer layers, resulting in finer flour.

To produce large amounts of flour, the Romans used teams of animals to operate massive grinding stone wheels.

In Europe, by the Middle Ages, there was a thriving bakery trade with specialist bakers producing whole-grain traditional loaves as well as more-refined and luxurious white bread. Loaves were produced to suit all levels of society: "hall" bread for the property

Maize was the staple grain known to Native Americans, so they used it to make flat breads. They often used a metate, a Mesoamerican flat mortar, to grind the corn into a flour.

owners made from the finest milled grain; hulled bread, made from bran, for the servants; well-cooked, crusty whole wheat (known as wholemeal in the UK) loaves for cooking; and trenchers, which were thick, dense, flat breads used as a plate during medieval feasts—after the platter contents had been consumed, the leftover trencher was soaked by the juices from the meal and was either eaten at the table or given away to the poor.

Fancy breads and pastries became popular during the Renaissance period, and domestic recipes began to appear in cookbooks of the time. During the eighteenth century, agricultural systems further evolved. Cereals could be more refined and ground, and the introduction of silk sieves produced a finer, powdery form of flour. Bakers were able to use brewers' and distillers' yeasts as ingredients, adding them directly to bread mixtures rather than the traditional method of adding a piece of fermented dough to achieve a rise.

In America, Native Americans were making flat breads from corn, also known as maize. This was the only grain available to them until early settlers arrived from Europe and

The origin of tandoor bread, bread made in a traditional clay oven, is unknown. But it dates back 5,000 years during the Indus Valley Civilization, located in the region we know today as South Asia.

brought with them wheat and rye, which thrived.

The newcomers found that their flours combined well with cornmeal to make different types of loaves. Influxes of various European immigrants helped increase the variety of baked goods as each settler brought with them their own country's recipes. Scandinavians used rye flour to make limpa, a yeast-leavened spice loaf, while the Germans used rye to make rich, dark pumpernickel bread. Italians from Naples introduced the bread-based pizza, and the Dutch, doughnuts

As civilizations evolved, water then wind was harnessed to turn the stones in purpose-built mills. In modern industrial times, purpose-built mills like windmills were constructed to grind wheat for flour.

and waffles. The prospectors and explorers who arrived in the West in the nineteenth century brought with them their sourdough techniques, and today sourdough bread is synonymous with San Francisco.

Wheat has been growing in northern China for a long time but was mainly eaten by the more affluent in society. Most of the population ate millet and barley among other grains. In this part of the world, the baking oven was not known, and so bread and similar foods were steamed. In Japan, rice was the crop of choice and was simply eaten as a grain. However, after a succession of famines in the nineteenth century, bakers became more interested in making bread; although it was drier, sweeter, and more cake-like than more familiar Western breads.

In India, wheat was common in the north but was expensive, so various grains and other cereals were used to make flours for baking. Clay ovens, called tandoors, have been used to make crisp, chewy, and bubbly naan bread for many years, but most flat breads from this part of Asia are cooked on simple flat stones and griddle-type flat plates.

The Industrial Revolution in the eighteenth and nineteenth centuries in Europe and North America brought with it huge social changes. Work took people outside their own homes and personal incomes increased. People left rural areas and moved to towns and cities, and to meet demand, the bakery business expanded and became mechanized on a large scale. In the 1870s, steel roller mills arrived, and white flour was able to be produced on a huge scale and old coal ovens were replaced with more efficient gas ovens, which helped speed up the baking process.

By the twentieth century, advances in the breadmaking process were evolving more rapidly. Flour was bleached, seemingly to make it more appealing, and the requirement to enrich flour with calcium, iron, and vitamins was introduced. After the second World War, once rationing was over, the consumption of foods high in fat and sugar rose in popularity, and baking bread became a factory operation.

The most notable development happened in 1961, when the Chorleywood bread process (CBP) was launched. This sped up the whole industry by developing a factory procedure that was able to use lower-grade wheat, more yeast, and more chemical ingredients in combination with rapid fermentation and high-speed

With advancements in technology during the twentieth century, mills were able to speed up the breadmaking process by using industrial grinders to make flour.

mechanized dough mixing. CBP was adopted by many countries around the world; the resulting bread was softer and less crusty and was easily available and affordable. This mass-produced bread was easy to eat and provided easy sustenance for people on the move. In the home, the bread lasted several days and provided a cheap filler to bulk out more-expensive foods like meat, fish, and dairy products. As more and more women went out to work, they had less time to make their own loaves, and most people became reliant on commercially produced bread.

Just a few decades later, a resurgence in baking would begin again. Once we all became more concerned about what we were eating in relation to our health, there was a drive to reduce fat, sugar, and salt in our diet. Consumers began to demand better flavor, texture, and quality from their daily bread. Concern about the use of pesticides in wheat production,

The development of the Chorleywood bread process (CBP) in 1961 resulted in mass-produced bread that was softer, easier to eat, affordable, and lasted several days at room temperature.

and artificial additives used during commerical breadmaking, prompted a return to more-traditional types of flour as well as a rise in the production of organic cereals. Advances in medical research helped diagnose Celiac (Coeliac) disease, which is an individual's intolerance to wheat and gluten. Manufacturers began to change the way they produced bread, and more organic, less-refined, and gluten-free loaves appeared on the shelves at local bakeries and grocery stores.

In the 1980s, a domestic mechanical bread machine was invented in Japan, and in a small way, this too contributed to the way we looked at our daily loaf. Soon, many homes embraced this appliance, which not only made and proved the dough from scratch, but also baked it as well. We were back to baking daily loaves, but in only a fraction of the time than making it by hand.

In recent years, artisan bakeries have sprung up, and more bakers are making bread to traditional recipes again. With the rise in popularity of farmers markets and specialist shops, bread has become more and more exotic and flavorsome. As is often the way, this sparks off an interest in the domestic setting, and once again, cooks have begun making their own bread from scratch.

While cooking was seen as a necessary evil a few years ago, taking up valuable leisure time and entertainment outside the home, in times of austerity and stress, home baking has become something that many of us enjoy. Never was this more apparent than during the worldwide pandemic in 2020. More and more of us spent time in our kitchens during lockdown, experimenting with recipes that we didn't usually have time to make. The rise in veganism across the world and increase in environmental concerns have also helped increase the interest in making bread from scratch. Many bread recipes are naturally vegan, and those that aren't can usually be adapted to become vegan-friendly.

Breadmaking has become so popular now that it has developed its own personality across all forms of social media with individuals sharing images, techniques, and recipes of their prized loaves. On television, shows based around baking challenges are fascinating audiences all over the world. There can be no doubt that we are enjoying baking bread more than ever before, and we are creating all sorts of delicious variations using the wealth of ingredients we have available to us today.

Household appliance companies have created easy-to-use and time-efficient bread maker machines for those who wish to make homemade bread.

Yeast is the most commonly used leavening agent for making bread. Its three standard forms are shown here: fresh, active dry, and instant dry.

Essential Ingredients

The archetypal loaf is made from flour, water, yeast, and a little seasoning. The type of flour you use along with other variations in ingredients will affect the outcome of your bread. The following pages offer a comprehensive guide to the different types of flour, leavening agents, and liquids you can use, as well as other ingredients that can be added to enrich, flavor, and give texture to your bakes.

To reduce the risks to the health of the wheat crops and the surrounding environment, sustainable farming methods have been encouraged, such as less reliance on artificial fertilizers to raise production levels.

Wheat

Today, wheat is one of the most important crops grown globally and is a vital ingredient for most breads and bakery items. To many of us, seeing fields of uniform wheat stems swaying gently in the breeze is a familiar and comforting sight. Over the past 200 years or so, farming has changed dramatically as demand for wheat has increased. More land has been taken over for raising crops, soil is fertilized before sowing to encourage growth, and crops are sprayed with pesticides and herbicides to prevent pests and diseases as well as to restrict weed growth. These practices, over time, cause a lack of biodiversity in soil and carbon escape when the soil is tilled, and this leads to an overall negative impact on the surrounding environment, wildlife, and human health.

However, new practices are being developed and adopted all the time to help reduce the

Before the invention of the combine harvester, wheat grass was cut by hand with simple farming hand tools, such as a sickle.

risks to the environment and health. More sustainable methods are being encouraged, and subsequently, crops will benefit from growing in a healthier, more-natural ecosystem and environment—one that is not reliant on artificial fertilizers and other controls to raise production levels.

The wheat crop is most usually planted in winter or spring. It is harvested in the late summer to early autumn. For centuries, the basic harvesting process remained unchanged. Wheat stalks were reaped (cut) using a long, curved blade and the stems gathered in sheaves. Once collected, the wheat was threshed to loosen the edible grain from the chaff (protective casing) and was then winnowed (air sifted) to get rid of the chaff altogether.

Up until the invention of the combine harvester in the nineteenth century, these processes were carried out by hand or simple mechanical methods. As harvesting has become increasingly mechanized, crop production can be carried out in a much shorter period, using much less manual labor. Today, modern vehicles have GPS tracking and laser-guided steering to make harvesting as efficient as possible.

Since its invention in the nineteenth century, the combine harvester has been used by farmers to efficiently harvest large amounts of wheat.

The Wheat Grain

It helps to know a little about the wheat grain and its composition before you choose your flour. Wheat contains more protein than rice and most other cereals. It supplies the body with all the amino acids it needs, though some in much smaller quantities than others. However, in combination with a diet containing animal and dairy products, or pulses if you are vegan, the right nutritional balance can easily be achieved.

Wheat grain supplies the body with an abundance of amino acids and contains more protein than rice and most other grains.

The bran is the husky, fibrous, outer part of the grain, and the germ is the nutritious seed. Right in the center is the endosperm, which is full of the starch and protein that makes up the bulk of flour. While there are several different proteins in the endosperm, the two most important for breadmaking are gliadin and glutenin. They are insoluble, and when they get stirred up in a mixture with liquid, they produce the sticky substance gluten, which gives elasticity to bread dough and helps hold up the basic structure of the loaf during cooking. Wheat flour made from varieties of wheat with a protein content of 12% or more will make the best-textured bread. These high protein flours contain more of the proteins that make gluten and are made from hard grain varieties of wheat.

ANATOMY OF A GRAIN

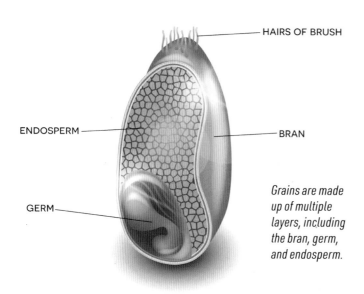

HAIRS OF BRUSH

ENDOSPERM

BRAN

GERM

Grains are made up of multiple layers, including the bran, germ, and endosperm.

Wheat Flours

Milling is the process that transforms the wheat grain into the flour we use for baking. You will notice on some bags of flour the term "stoneground." This means that the wheat has been crushed between two large flat stones, and the resulting flour usually retains all three parts of the grain. At this stage, the flour is whole wheat. Once sifted, the main fibrous parts are removed, and the resulting flour is powdery and beige to gray in color, as it still retains some of the bran particles.

If a bag of flour doesn't mention the word "stoneground," then it has been roller milled. Roller milling is the general method used in flour production; it crushes grains into a powder through a series of steel rollers. White flour is usually roller milled.

There are many varieties of wheat flour available at grocery stores, health food shops, and specialist suppliers. It can be quite a daunting task working out which brand or variety to choose for your specific bread. Compositions can vary considerably, so take a little time to read the packet to try and obtain as much information about the type of flour you are buying before you start your breadmaking. Here are a few general types of wheat flour explained:

All-Purpose (Plain) White Flour—A traditional, multipurpose wheat flour milled from soft grain wheat varieties with a protein content between 7% and 10%. This flour is best kept for cake and pastry making, or for making softer, unleavened breads where a spongy, lighter texture is required. In some recipes, all-purpose flour is mixed with a more traditional bread flour to give a softer crumb.

Whole Wheat (Wholemeal) All-Purpose (Plain) Flour—This nutritious flour contains all the grain, bran, and germ of the wheat kernel. It has more protein than its refined white cousin; the protein comes from the germ protein rather than from gluten. Therefore, use this flour in the same way as all-purpose white flour to add a slightly more fibrous texture and nuttier flavor.

Bread Flour—Also called strong and very strong bread flour. This is the flour of choice for breadmaking and is available as white flour or whole wheat flour. These flours are made from hard wheat varieties, which naturally contain more gluten. Overall protein content is between 12% and 14%, depending on the manufacturer, with some as high as 17%. **Whole wheat bread flour** is made with the whole wheat kernel and has more fiber. Using all whole wheat bread flour to make a loaf will give a dense, heavy texture because the extra bran content inhibits gluten development during kneading. Therefore, you may want to experiment by combining white and whole wheat to obtain an acceptable texture—see some suggested ratios on page 28.

Brown Flour—Also called wheatmeal. This is a lighter, less fiber-rich version of whole wheat flour, with some of the wheat bran removed. It contains most of the wheat germ so is still of good nutritional quality. It will make a lighter loaf than one made with whole wheat.

Soft-Grain Bread Flour—White bread flour with added kibbled or cracked wheat and rye grains, which add texture. This flour makes an excellent halfway measure in the effort to increase dietary fiber in the diet without the heaviness and overt nutrition achieved by using 100-percent whole wheat flour, and most kids find it acceptable as well!

Granary Malted Brown Bread Flour—Also called country grain, malted wheat grain, and malthouse flour. A delicious bread flour with added malted wheat flakes, which give a nutty texture and sweet flavor.

Semolina Flour—Can be coarsely ground or finely ground when it is known as durum flour. This is the flour used in pasta making. It is milled from durum wheat, which is one of the hardest varieties. It is a pale, creamy gold in color, and when mixed with white bread flour, it makes a slightly coarser-textured, more rustic loaf with good flavor and creamier-colored crumb.

Spelt Flour—Also called hulled wheat or dinkel wheat, this flour is now widely available. It is made from an ancient grain dating back to Roman times. *Triticum spelta* wheat has different gluten components than many of the modern-day commercial wheat varieties, and as such, some people find it easier to digest. When spelt grain is milled, the resulting flour is lighter than traditional whole wheat flour. You will also find a white spelt flour that has the fibrous

Wheat flour comes in many variations, such as granary (1), white bread (2), spelt (3), Khorasan (4), whole wheat (5), and soft grain (6).

parts of the grain removed. The different protein balance in the spelt grain means that the gluten is less stretchy and subsequently makes a cakier-textured loaf. However, the flavor is delicious with a slightly nutty taste. The texture can be improved by mixing it with white bread flour if preferred.

Einkorn Flour—*Triticum monococcum* is one of the oldest wheat varieties to be cultivated. It thrives in poor soil conditions where other varieties are unable to flourish. It is genetically different from other wheat, and the grains grow singly on either side of the stem, hence the name "ein," meaning one in German. The flour looks like whole wheat and can be used as such. It is lower in starch than other wheat and gives a denser, more rustic texture. It has around 15% protein and a higher proportion of vitamin B, minerals, and dietary fiber. It gives an earthy flavor to bakes.

Emmer Flour—*Triticum dicoccum* is a relative of einkorn and durum wheat. It is also known as farro. The wheat grows very tall, which makes it more challenging to harvest, but it tolerates drought and is more resistant to pests than other varieties and as such is becoming more widely available. Like spelt, it is also more easily digested by individuals with a slight wheat intolerance. Emmer flour is more cream colored than the other whole wheat flours and adds a buttery, wheaty flavor. It is best mixed with another wheat flour.

Khorasan Flour—*Triticum turanicum* is another ancient grain dating back to ancient Egypt; it is also known as KAMUT® (Egyptian for wheat). This whole wheat flour is paler in color and milder in flavor. It has a higher protein content, but the gluten produced is less suitable for breadmaking on its own. For the best results, mix it with standard wheat flour.

Nonwheat Flours

No other cereal crop contains as much vital gluten as wheat, but ever since breadmaking began, people have been grinding up other grains and cereals to mix with wheat flour to add variety, flavor, and different textures to their baking.

Rye Flour—A hardy grain that tolerates wet and cold climates, hence its popularity in Russian, Scandinavian, and North European cookery. It contains some gluten, and when used on its own, it will make a very heavy-textured bread with a distinctly acidic flavor. For most palates, it is better mixed with wheat flour for a lighter loaf.

Barley Flour—Once the husky bran is removed from barley grains, it becomes pearl or pot barley, which is a familiar ingredient in stews and soups. Pearl barley is ground to make a

Similar to wheat flour, there are many varieties of nonwheat flours on the market, including oat (1), soya (2), buckwheat (3), gram (4), white rice (5), and rye (6).

delicious, sweet, earthy flour. It contains low levels of gluten so is not suitable for a gluten-free diet. It gives a dense texture when used on its own and is best mixed with wheat flour.

Buckwheat Flour—Also known as beech wheat, brank, or Saracen corn. These grayish, triangular grains come from a plant native to Russia that is related to rhubarb, not wheat. Buckwheat is a gluten-free, nutritious grain, containing the bioflavonoid rutin that is used as a natural remedy for circulatory problems. When ground into flour, it has a nutty, earthy flavor. It should be mixed with wheat flour for making bread. In gluten-free baking, adding buckwheat provides extra flavor to a loaf.

Oat Flour—Cleaned and hulled oat grains are called "grouts," and these can be ground finely to make a tasty, nutritious, and fiber-rich flour. Pure uncontaminated oats are naturally gluten-free, but often oats are processed on premises where other gluten-containing grains are handled. If you have Celiac disease, always read the product label for suitability. Oat flour can be mixed with wheat flour to give a richer, slightly chewier texture to a loaf.

Quinoa Flour—A very high-protein grain with a high concentration of amino acids. It hails from South America where it is a very valuable crop and grows at altitudes too high for maize. It is naturally gluten-free, creamy beige in color, but has little flavor. It is used with other flours in breadmaking to enhance the nutritional quality of the finished loaf.

Chickpea Flour—Also called gram flour and garbanzo bean flour. It is made from grinding chickpeas into a golden, powdery flour. It contains no gluten and has a rich earthy, beany flavor that is best suited to savory breads. In Indian cooking, it is used to make pancakes, bhajis, and flat breads. A little goes a long way when mixed with other flours to give a unique, rich, earthy flavor.

Potato Flour—A very starchy, pure-white, grainy flour made from potato starch. It contains no gluten and is used in small quantities with bread flour to soften a loaf and give a moist texture.

Soya Flour—Milled from soybeans, this flour has a very high protein content; it is low in carbohydrates, contains no gluten, and is used to enhance the nutritional content of a loaf. It also adds a creamier, softer texture to the crumb. Mixed into a paste with water, it is also used as a vegan egg-replacement glaze (page 34).

Cornmeal or Maizemeal—Widely used as a staple grain in corn- or maize-growing parts of the world. It varies in texture from very fine (masa harina) to coarse (polenta). It can be made from white, yellow, or blue corn and has a gritty texture that varies depending on how finely ground it is. It contains no gluten. It is often added to wheat flours in breadmaking but also mixed with other nongluten flours to make dense, soda-style breads. It will add color and a sweet flavor to your baking.

Cornmeal can have a coarse texture, like this polenta.

Cornstarch—Also called cornflour in the UK. This is the finest-ground form of corn or maize. It is a silky white powder, packed full of starch, and mostly used to thicken sauces. In breadmaking, it helps achieve a finer crumb. In gluten-free baking, cornstarch can help bind a mixture together and gives a slightly chewier texture; it has no flavor. Use with other flours rather than as a flour on its own.

Rice Flour—Finely ground white or brown rice grains are used to make this variety of flour. It is very starchy, contains no gluten, and used in small amounts to lighten and soften the crumb. Brown rice flour will add a little nutty flavor. Rice flour is the mainstay of most gluten-free baking, as it adds bulk to a recipe. Glutinous rice flour is made from the rice used to make sweet "sticky" rice dishes popular in parts of Asia. Despite its name, it contains no gluten. In gluten-free baking, the very starchy texture of the cooked flour helps provide a chewier texture in steamed breads. Use it as part of a flour blend rather than as a flour on its own.

Tapioca Flour—Also called cassava, manioc, and yuca. This flour is made from the elongated root of a tropical plant that is a staple in northern South America, Africa, and parts of Asia. It is made into flatbread and can be used after it has been fermented. It is a white powdery, gluten-free flour and is extremely starchy. It makes a good addition to gluten-free bakes by adding bulk and a chewier texture, but it is too dense to be used on its own and should be used as part of a flour blend.

Making Your Own Bread Flour Blends

For the best results, use at least one-half bread flour in your loaf. If the other half of the flour quantity is made with gluten-free flour, the loaf will still rise, but the texture will be far less chewy and springy than your usual all-wheat loaf.

To avoid disappointment, for the inexperienced bread maker who wants to make a whole wheat loaf, start by making a loaf with one-half white bread flour and one-half whole wheat bread flour. This will give a lightly fibered loaf with a good rise and a chewy texture. For a denser texture, move on to three-quarters whole wheat to one-quarter white bread flour. Once you have mastered this type of dough, you can try making one with all whole wheat bread flour.

Using a flour with a distinct flavor, such as gram, soya, buckwheat, and rye, is down to personal taste, but as a general rule, replacing 6–8 Tbsp. (45–60g) wheat flour with one of the above will make a subtle change to a large white loaf. **Note:** Because rye flour does contain gluten, it can be used in larger quantities than other nonwheat-grain flours, but the flavor is distinctly different and may not be as palatable if used in a higher ratio.

Flours like rice and potato, which are used to soften the texture of the crumb, and 4–6 Tbsp. (30–45g) wheat flour should be sufficient to make a subtle difference.

Gluten- and Wheat-Free All-Purpose and Bread Flour Blends

Several manufacturers have put together their own blends of gluten-free flours to make life easier for the consumer. Ready-blended combinations often include rice, buckwheat, corn, tapioca, and potato flour. Gluten-free flour labeled specifically for breadmaking includes a quantity of the natural binder xanthan gum (page 31). If you decide to use this type of flour, you will not need to add your own xanthan gum to the ingredients.

Loaves made with gluten-free flour will not be the same as the traditional wheat loaf; the recipes are quite different, both in ingredients and method. The resulting loaves will be denser in texture, more cake-like, and less crusty, but using gluten-free flour blends makes an excellent alternative to going without bread altogether and saves time and money putting your own combinations together.

Like many food alternatives for dietary restrictions, an increase in awareness creates an increase in demand. Gluten-free bread is available at many grocery stores, restaurants, and bakeries.

Yeast and Other Leavening Agents

Yeast is a leavening agent and is a main ingredient in most bread recipes. Yeast is available in three forms: fresh (1), active dry (2), and instant dry (3).

Using a leavening agent is an important part of most breads. This is the essential ingredient that helps create the airy gas (carbon dioxide) in the dough that makes the bread rise. In most bread recipes, yeast is the primary ingredient for this purpose. It is available in three different forms:

Fresh Yeast—Looks a bit like chunks of canned tuna. It is moist and soft in texture and smells fresh and slightly sweet. You may be able to obtain some from a local bakery, but you can also order it online. It is usually packaged in large blocks or smaller, individually wrapped portions. It is best used as soon as possible after purchase to ensure it is as fresh as possible. Keep it well wrapped up and in the fridge and use according to the use-by date. If you buy fresh yeast in bulk, cut it up into measured portions, wrap it securely in plastic wrap, and keep it frozen until you need it (up to six months). It thaws very quickly and becomes liquid once defrosted, but it can be activated in the same way as if it were fresh.

Active Dry Yeast—Also called dried yeast. Often packaged in resealable small jars or bags, this concentrated form of yeast will keep in a cool, dark cupboard for about two months once opened. It resembles tiny, yellow-brown seeds. Like fresh yeast, you need to mix it with warm liquid to activate it, and this process often takes slightly longer than when using fresh. If your recipe requires ½ oz. (15g) fresh yeast, use 2 teaspoons dried.

Instant Dry Yeast—Also called instant dry dried yeast, quick yeast, or fast-acting yeast. This yeast is finer than active dry yeast and has been specially formulated to need no reactivating. It is added directly to the flour *before* the liquid is added to make the dough, otherwise it won't work. This yeast is most often available in ready-to-use, one-portion ¼ oz. (7g) sachets—equivalent to just over 2 teaspoons—and as such is equivalent to ½ oz. (15g) fresh yeast or 2 teaspoons active dry, but always check the manufacturer's guidelines for any variations. Once opened, it loses its potency quickly. It is best stored in a clean, airtight container in a cool, dry place. Refer to the recommended use-by date once opened.

Starters

There are many recipes and methods for this natural method of making bread rise. It is a lengthier process (usually around three to five days) than using other leavening agents, but once a starter is made, it can be replenished. Providing it is stored correctly, you will have a continuous supply for your breadmaking. Loaves made with a starter have a fresh, light, acidic flavor and often have a more-aerated crumb. The longer the starter is left to mature, the more acidic the flavor.

Flour and water are the basic ingredients, and yeast is added to help ferment the mixture, although starters can be made completely yeast-free. Once made, store your starter in a sealable container in the fridge. There is a basic recipe that has been used in conjunction with the relevant recipes in this book on page 49. Traditional French bread recipes are made with a starter called *poolish*

Using a yeast starter is the most-natural method for making bread rise, but it typically takes a few days to make.

(page 99) and Italy has a similar starter called *biga* (page 102). These starters are made over a shorter period and give a milder, less-acidic tang to the breads they are added to.

You will also find sachets of ready-made starter mixes available. These contain the basic ingredients you need to get a starter going. All you need to do is add liquid and follow the manufacturer's instructions.

Other Leavening Agents

While most bread doughs use yeast to give them a light and airy texture, some recipes for quick breads or those formulated for anyone on a yeast-free diet use other chemical leaveners to aerate a mixture. They are usually stirred into the dry ingredients before the liquid is added. Once moistened, these agents get to work quickly, releasing the gases that help the mixture rise. For maximum benefit, you should aim to bake the mixture quickly before the aeration is lost.

Baking Powder—A commercial mix of alkaline, baking soda, and acidic cream of tartar, which is combined with a dried starch, wheat, or rice flour to stabilize them. They react together in the presence of moisture to make carbon dioxide gas, which helps the mixture rise. You can make your own baking powder by mixing one tablespoon baking soda with

Baking soda is a yeast alternative. When combined with an acidic ingredient, such as lemon juice, it produces carbon dioxide, which helps the mixture rise.

two teaspoons cream of tartar. Always measure using level spoon measurements unless otherwise stated—too much or too little can upset the balance of the recipe. If you're on a gluten-free diet, make sure you buy a wheat-free product.

Baking Soda (Sodium Bicarbonate)—This alkaline substance can be used on its own in a mixture where an acidic ingredient is present, e.g., buttermilk or lemon juice. This will help produce the same reaction achieved by using baking powder. It is worth noting that baking soda has a salty flavor, so you may want to reduce the seasoning in your mixture if adding baking soda or baking powder to your recipe.

Texture Improvers for Gluten-Free Baking

Xanthan Gum—Also known as corn sugar gum, it has a food additive reference number of E415. This rather scientific-sounding ingredient gets its name from a group of bacteria that are used in the fermentation process. The bacteria form a natural, slimy substance, and this has been formulated for culinary use. Xanthan gum is widely used in gluten-free recipes to help improve crumb structure by acting as a binding agent. In breadmaking, xanthan gum powder is mixed into gluten-free flour before the yeast and any liquid is added. You should be able to buy xanthan gum from large grocery stores, health food stores, sellers of special diet products, and online. Always refer to the manufacturer's guidelines for quantity, but generally in breadmaking, use 1 teaspoon per 9 oz. (250g) gluten-free flour.

Psyllium Husk Powder—Derives from a shrub-like herb called *Plantago psyllium*, which grows most predominantly in India. The husk is the outer coating of the psyllium seed. It's a rich source of fiber, making it a popular choice as a supplement for improved gut health. When mixed with water, it turns into a gloopy, sticky mixture that greatly helps improve the texture of gluten-free bread mixtures. Available from health food shops and online, make sure you buy the powdered form for baking. Like xanthan gum, it is mixed into the dry ingredients before liquid is added. Follow your recipe's instructions for quantity, but as a rough guideline, use ½ oz. (15g) per 7 oz. (200g) gluten-free flour.

Psyllium husk powder and xanthan gum can be used to improve texture in gluten-free breads.

Liquids like water, milk, and sometimes juice are all useful liquids to bind the flour together to make gluten. Alternative, plant-based milks, like oat milk, are a great dairy-free option.

Other Ingredients

Liquid

The third key ingredient in breadmaking is liquid. This helps bind the mixture by bringing the flour together to make a stiff paste and develop gluten. It is either a carrier for adding yeast to the mixture or an activator to help the leavening process to get started. Water is the most used, and it gives the most chewy, familiar texture to a loaf. Dairy or plant-based milk can be used. The fat content of the added liquid determines the texture of the finished crumb, e.g., the higher the fat, the more cake-like the crumb. Fruit and vegetable juices can be used as the liquid in breadmaking, but you need to be mindful of the extra sugar you will be adding to the dough and make any adjustments to your recipe as necessary.

Salt

As well as being an obvious flavor enhancer, salt acts as a brake mechanism in breadmaking. It prevents the yeast from overworking, which would cause the dough to collapse. Salt inhibits fermentation and helps gluten to develop and strengthen, which in turn forms the structure of the loaf. Always measure out salt carefully to avoid adding too much, and use natural sea salts rather than salt substitutes. Choose a finely ground salt or salt flakes rather than coarsely ground, as it dissolves more quickly.

Sugar

A lot of recipes, savory as well as sweet, contain a sweetening agent in the form of sugars, honey, maple, corn syrups, malt extract, treacle, or molasses. Traditionally, sugar is used to fuel yeast and speed up the fermentation process, but in fact, bread dough doesn't need any sugar to get working. However, adding a little will help develop flavor, texture, and help to form the bread crust. If your recipe requires sugar, measure the amount carefully as too much sweetness can prevent the yeast from working properly. Specially formulated sweet bread recipes are often heavier in texture than more traditional-style loaves.

Fat

A small amount of fat is sometimes added to breads to improve texture and flavor by slightly enriching the dough, but many breads are made without adding any fat at all. In very rich mixtures like Brioche (page 132), the fat is added after the dough has been formed. The more fat that is added to a mixture, the more the fat coats the strands of gluten, slowing down fermentation and the dough's capacity to rise.

Precise measurements of ingredients are crucial for baking, and baking bread is no different. Always measure with your equipment instead of guessing for best results.

Unsalted dairy or plant butters (choose unsalted to prevent overseasoning), lard, shortening, white vegetable fat, and vegetable oils are all used in breadmaking. Reduced-fat spreads are less reliable because of their increased water content and are best avoided unless specifically required in your recipe. If using a vegan alternative to butter, make sure that fat content is at least 79% for best results.

Extras and Additions

Once you've got the breadmaking bug, you'll want to experiment with different recipes and add your favorite ingredients to the tried-and-tested ones. There are plenty of "extras" that can be added to doughs to give more flavor, color, and health benefits, as well as change the texture. Here are some to consider:

Egg and Vegan Egg

Adding egg increases the nutritional content of a loaf as well as giving it more color and a richer texture. Always use fresh, free-range, or organic eggs for the best flavor and color, and use them at room temperature. Remember that using egg will increase the liquid volume of your recipe, so break them into a bowl and beat lightly, then top up with liquid to the stated amount in the recipe.

There are several ready-made vegan egg alternatives available to buy. Always follow the manufacturer's recommendations before using in a recipe. The recipes in this book have been tested using a simple flax-based substitute. For every medium egg—2 oz. (50g) beaten—equivalent, mix 1 Tbsp. finely ground flax seed with 3 Tbsp. (45mL) cold water, and leave for a few minutes until thickened, then use as directed in the recipe.

Dairy Products and Plant-Based Alternatives

As well as using milk as the liquid in breadmaking, you can enrich a loaf further by replacing some of the liquid with natural or plain dairy, plant-based yogurts, evaporated milk,

Eggs or vegan eggs, like flax-based substitutes, can be used to enrich a dough, adding nutritional content, a deliciously rich texture, and a light-golden color.

buttermilk, and unflavored soft cheese products (fromage frais, quark, or cottage cheese). For a very rich texture, you can use small amounts of full-fat soft cheeses like mascarpone or cream cheese; and half-and-half, light, light whipping, heavy whipping, or plant-based creams. The higher the fat content of the product you add, the more close-textured and less risen your loaf will be. Added correctly, small amounts of dairy product will enhance the moisture of the bread crumb and enrich the flavor.

Cheese—A very popular additional ingredient to savory and some sweet doughs. Grated cheese can be added at the beginning of the breadmaking, mixed into the flour, so it can be thoroughly incorporated to give a rounded, savory flavor. You can also add cheese when you are kneading the bread, and this will show as distinct pieces of cheese in your finished loaf. It can also be sprinkled on top of your loaf before baking to make a cheesy crust.

Choose a well-flavored cheese for best results, one that will add good savoriness in a small amount; for example, Parmesan, sharp (farmhouse or mature) cheddar, Roquefort, or Stilton. Remember that many cheeses are quite salty, so you may need to reduce the amount of additional seasoning in your recipe. Adding too much cheese to your bread dough will result in a soft dough. Remember, the cheese will melt and increase the liquid and fat content, so weigh it out accurately, and don't be tempted to over-cheese the dough!

Vegan Cheese—If you want to experiment with dairy alternatives in your breadmaking, choose a firmer-textured cheese substitute like an Italian hard cheese or Parmesan equivalent, so you won't need to add too great a quantity to enhance the flavor of your dough. Be mindful of the ingredients used in the making of your chosen cheese and how their flavor may affect the finished bread. For example, a coconut milk–based cheese will add quite a distinct flavor to your loaf. Check the product details to see that it is heat stable and suitable for cooking before using it in your recipe.

Tofu—Firm varieties of tofu, especially smoked tofu, make an interesting and nutritious addition to a savory loaf. Grate the tofu and work it into the dough as you would for grated cheese. Silken and soft tofu can be blended into the liquid quantity required to make up your loaf to help increase the protein content of a bread. The texture of the loaf will be denser.

Other Additions

Fiber—Many loaves of bread are already a good source of dietary fiber, but you can increase the nutritional content further by adding an extra ingredient. If you find 100-percent whole wheat bread just a bit too virtuous, you could try adding a source of dietary fiber to a standard white bread flour. Extra liquid is often required when adding extra ingredients, as increased fiber absorbs more moisture than flour. Adding too much bran fiber will inhibit gluten activity, so measure accurately. Here are some guidelines:

- **Wheat and Oat Bran**—Excellent source of fiber but add no more than 2 Tbsp. (7g) per 8 oz. (225g) flour.
- **Wheatgerm**—A good source of vitamin E and adds a delicious mild nutty flavor. Use 2 Tbsp. (7g) per 8 oz. (225g) flour.
- **Rolled Oats**—Add plain or lightly toasted to a dough to give a chewier texture and slightly nutty flavor. Use 2 Tbsp. (20g) per 8 oz. (225g) flour.
- **Unsweetened Muesli**—Combinations of chopped nuts, vine fruits, and cereals add flavor, texture, and nutritional quality to your loaf. Use 2 Tbsp. (20g) per 8 oz. (225g) flour.
- **Cooked Brown or Wild Rice**—An excellent choice for gluten-free breads. Rice will help keep the bread dough moist. It also adds fiber, texture, and a nutty flavor to your finished loaf. Use 2 oz. (50g) per 8 oz. (225g) flour.

Nuts and Seeds—Small whole or chopped nuts and seeds can be added to the flour at the beginning of a sweet or savory loaf recipe for texture and flavor. You can also replace some of the cereal flour in a recipe with finely ground nuts—ground almonds, chestnuts, toasted hazelnuts, and unsweetened coconut add flavor and a delicious richness to a loaf, also perfect for gluten-free cooking. Remember that nuts and seeds are rich in oils, and adding a ground nut "flour" to a mixture will increase the fat content and affect the rise of the dough. Replace 4–6 Tbsp. (30–45g) of the flour in your recipe with finely ground nuts or seeds for best results. Expect the dough to be denser and close-crumbed, but the flavor and nutritional value will be enhanced.

Chocolate—Melted chocolate can be mixed into your chosen liquid at the start of the breadmaking process, but be mindful that you are also adding fat and sugar to your mixture. Alternatively, you can stir cocoa powder into the flour as you would when making a chocolate cake. Small chunks of chocolate or chocolate chips can be added when kneading the dough to give small pockets of molten chocolate when the bread is freshly baked.

Fruit and Vegetables—All these prepared fruit and vegetables can be added to breads to make some interesting colors, flavors, and textures: grated raw and cooked vegetables; soaked, finely chopped, dried vegetables (use the soaking liquid in your recipe as well for extra flavor); small, dried vine fruits; chopped dried or candied fruit pieces; mashed or grated cooked root vegetables (beetroot, parsnip, carrot, or potato); tinned and drained or thawed frozen sweetcorn; chopped, stoned olives; mashed ripe banana; small fresh berries; finely chopped or grated apple or pear; or stewed or puréed cooked fruit.

The texture will often be heavier by adding a wet ingredient, so be mindful of the extra water content when using fresh fruit and vegetables that may make the dough more sticky and wet. The extra bulk from the added ingredient will also inhibit the rise of the bread. Try and find a reference recipe to base your experiments on to avoid disappointment.

Various additives can be added to bread to enhance the color, flavor, or textures, such as chocolate and cocoa powder (1), olives (2), nuts and seeds (3), dried fruit (4), and candied (glacé) cherries (5).

Meat—To make a very savory bread, delicious on a picnic or packed lunch, chop up small or mince pieces of cold cooked meat, such as chorizo, salami, smoked bacon, or ham. Stir into the flour at the beginning of your recipe. Use in small quantities to make sure the rise of the dough is not affected by the additional ingredients added.

Other Seasonings—There are all sorts of small ingredients you can add to make your bread extra tasty: dried and freshly chopped herbs; finely chopped fresh or dried chilies; ground spices or crushed whole spices (toast them lightly first for more depth of flavor); finely grated citrus rind; small pieces of preserved ginger; and good-quality flavor extracts and essences can be used to perk up your recipe. Dried herbs and ground spices add a more concentrated flavor than using freshly chopped herbs or grinding your own spices, so use them more sparingly.

One of the most popular flavors is garlic. Fresh garlic has antifungal properties and can inhibit the function of yeast. Always use fresh garlic sparingly in bread doughs, and slightly increasing the quantity of yeast you use can help reduce any possible antifungal effects. Alternatively, try dried garlic products like powder, granules, or flakes, or replace the salt in your recipe with garlic-flavored salt.

The essential equipment for making bread includes many things that you already have in your kitchen: rolling pin, thermometer, measuring spoons, measuring cup, large mixing bowl, and wooden spoon.

Equipment

You really don't need much in the way of specialist equipment to make your own bread, but there are a few useful bits and pieces that will help you achieve better results. If you want to experiment beyond the basics, then there is, of course, a whole host of "extra" breadmaking paraphernalia available as well as dedicated bakeware for specific types of loaf if you get the baking bug and want to make more of an investment in extending your collection.

Baking Supplies

Measuring—For most baking, it is important to be able to weigh and measure your ingredients accurately, and breadmaking is no exception. You should use a set of weighing scales with a minimum weighing capacity of ½ oz. (15g). **Digital weighing scales** offer the most accurate measurements and mean that you can weigh liquid as well as dry ingredients.

A medium-size glass or plastic **measuring cup** and a set of **measuring spoons** are also helpful for accuracy. Remember, when using measuring spoons, the ingredient should be level with the rim of the spoon for complete accuracy. As with all cooking, use one set of measurements throughout the recipe, and don't switch between imperial and metric. Unless otherwise stated, all spoon measurements are level.

To accurately measure and weigh dry and liquid ingredients, use a weighing scale with a minimum weighing capacity of ½ oz (15g).

Thermometer—Not essential, but using a thermometer is a failsafe precaution when activating fresh and active dry yeast, and it enables you to achieve the correct liquid temperature (page 40). Once you have made bread a few times, you will get a feel for what is the correct liquid temperature.

Mixing Bowls—Large mixing bowls made of glass, porcelain, or plastic are best for breadmaking (metal can react with yeast) and will give you plenty of space to mix the dough. A large bowl will also allow plenty of space for the dough to rise.

Starter Jar—If you plan to make bread using a sourdough starter, it is worth investing in a large glass storage jar with a good sealing lid. A large Kilner® or mason jar used for preserving is a good choice, as it has a noncorrosive, tight-fitting seal, which is ideal for long-term storage of the starter in the refrigerator. Glass is the best material because it can be made more sterile than plastic.

Covering Your Dough—To cut down on using disposable plastic, use a clean piece of **cheesecloth** (muslin) or designated good-quality tea towel for covering dough during rising and proving. If you have a collection of bowls, you may be able to fit one over your mixing bowl to allow extra space for the dough to rise instead of using a cloth cover. A shower cap is also a good covering as it will seal snuggly around the top of a bowl.

Proving Baskets—Widely available ridged baskets of all shapes and sizes that support bread during proving. You simply flour them and place the dough inside, seam side up, until it is ready for baking. Gently flip the dough onto a prepared baking tray and cook. The resulting bread should retain

Specialist or simple wicker baskets are often used to give bread a good shape as it proves, and a clean cheesecloth makes the perfect light covering when proving most breads.

the ridged basket pattern once the loaf is baked. Not an essential tool, but if you want an even, more-professional finish, the basket will help you achieve this. Alternatively, you can use an ordinary breadbasket, about 8" (20cm) diameter, lined with cheesecloth (muslin) or a clean tea towel in the same way.

Utensils—A **wooden spoon** and a clean pair of hands are all you need for mixing, but a **dough scraper** may be useful if you find mixtures sticking to the work surface. These range from simple thin pieces of flexible plastic to more substantial steel blades with wooden or plastic handles. A **wooden rolling pin** is helpful if you plan to make flatter loaves, but you can achieve quite a thin dough by pushing and pressing with your hands. A **bread lame** is basically a very thin sharp blade (often a razor blade) that attaches to a wooden or plastic handle. It is used to slash the top of the dough before baking to allow gases to escape; it also helps give a "designer" finish to your loaf. You can use a small sharp knife, but make sure the blade is thin so that it makes a clean cut rather than dragging through the dough, which may result in a more uneven incision. A **pastry brush** is an important tool if you want to glaze your loaves with an egg wash (beaten egg) or other finishes before and after baking. Make sure the brush ends are soft so that glazes can be applied easily and softly without damaging the dough. Silicone brushes are a good choice because they are soft, durable, and easy to clean. A small **sieve** is also useful if you want to finely dust flour or fine sugar on top of your loaves.

Pans and Bakeware—Good-quality bakeware is an important factor to help you achieve perfect loaves. It is worth investing in heavy-gauge baking pans and trays that are less likely

Good-quality, heavy-gauge baking pans and trays can make all the difference to your final bake, as they are less likely to warp in a hot oven.

to warp in the oven under the higher cooking temperatures required in breadmaking. To get you started, these supplies will be enough: a basic 2lb (900g) and 1lb (450g) loaf pan; a good-quality 7"–8" (18–20cm) diameter, 3" (7.5cm) deep, round cake pan; and a sturdy baking tray for individual rolls or a free-formed loaf. Once you have more experience, you may want to invest in other shaped pans, such as a perforated baguette tray.

Wire Rack—Once your bread is baked, you need to turn it out of the pan or transfer it to a wire rack to cool. The rack allows air to circulate round the loaf completely, cooling it more quickly and helping steam to escape, which keeps the crust crisp.

Bread Board and Knife—When your loaf is cool and ready to serve, a wooden board is the best surface for slicing bread. Keep the board just for bread to avoid transference of flavors. Use a large, serrated-edge knife for cutting. You'll find the slicing action is tolerated best by cutting on a wooden surface.

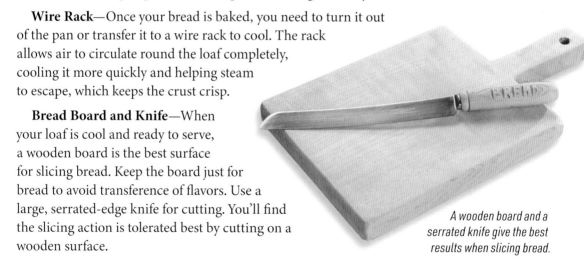

A wooden board and a serrated knife give the best results when slicing bread.

Appliances

If you have the budget and the kitchen space, you can lighten your workload by letting an electrical appliance do the mixing and kneading for you. Some hand mixers have special dough beaters, and food processors often have a plastic blade for mixing bread dough. A free-standing heavy-duty mixer is the ultimate in labor saving gadgets and will happily churn away your bread dough with a special hook designed for the job, and fully develop the elasticity of the dough while you get on with something else. Always refer to the manufacturer's instructions for specific guidelines, settings, and fittings for making bread doughs. Only use an appliance if the manufacturer states it is suitable for breadmaking to avoid overheating the appliance or damaging it with prolonged use and follow the instruction manual for running time.

When using a free-standing heavy-duty mixer to mix and knead the bread dough, make sure to use a dough hook attachment.

There can be no doubt that the introduction of the domestic electronic bread maker, an appliance that makes a whole loaf from mixing and proving to baking, has helped increase interest in baking bread at home. Seen as a wonderful invention by many because it "works while you play," making bread in a machine is quite a different technique, and is not covered in this book. If you are curious though, it is always important to follow the manufacturer's instructions and the recipe leaflet that comes with your machine or refer to a specialist bread maker cookery book.

Increasingly, we are looking for ways to cut back on the amount of energy we use, and how we cook our bread and other bakes is important. With the popularity of small, fast-cooking worktop appliances like the air fryer and multi cooker, there are now ways and means of baking a loaf of bread, albeit a small one, without having to put it in your conventional oven at all. You'll find a recipe for air fryer bread on page 147. At the opposite extreme, for anyone

A bread machine can be an easy, efficient, and helpful way to make bread while you work on other activities.

who's really prepared to wait a while, there is a recipe for a loaf of bread cooked in a slow cooker (page 150).

If you are able to make a larger investment, you'll find all sorts of sophisticated and specialist ovens on the market: small countertop bread provers; bread and pizza ovens which sit on the work surface and are just big enough to cook a small loaf or a family pizza; conventional electric ovens with in-built steam settings which release wafts of steam during cooking to improve rise and finish of your bakes; as well as a multitude of outdoor wood-fired, gas-fired and multi-fueled bread and pizza ovens from small tabletop appliances to the more permanently sited clay oven-style, with a

Cooking a few buns or one small loaf of bread in an air fryer is more fuel-efficient than heating up a large conventional oven.

Tabletop and outdoor, portable pizza ovens are a great appliance for baking pizza dough for home pizza nights.

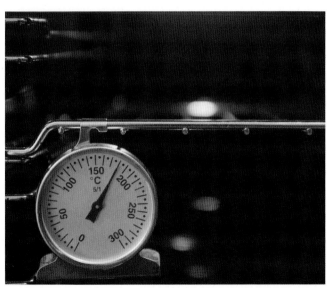

The temperature inside the oven might not always match what you set the oven to. Always double check with an oven thermometer.

whole host of portable devices in between.

For most of us, cooking bread by more conventional means is probably the most reliable way of achieving a perfectly acceptable loaf of bread. When you are more competent, batch baking is the best way to maximize oven space and fuel efficiency. Use an oven thermometer inside your oven to make sure the temperature inside matches the dial on the outside—you might be amazed at the difference between the two!

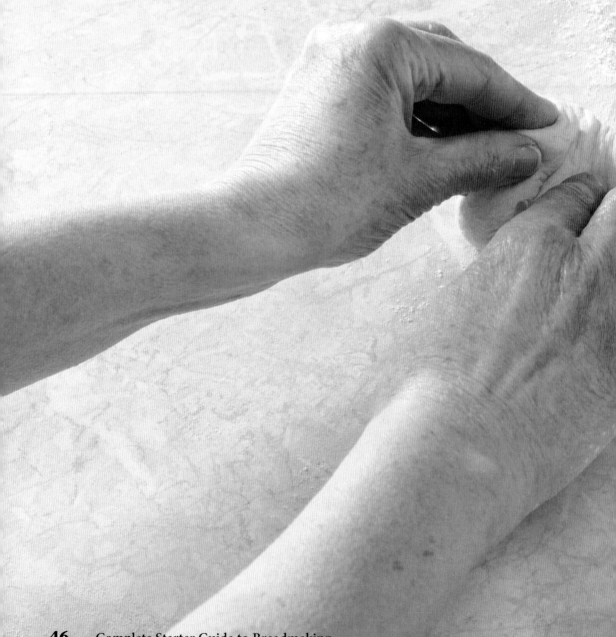

There are shaping techniques that have been developed over centuries. For example, baguettes and long loaves of bread need the ends need to be pinched in.

Basic Techniques

Now we've covered the ingredients and equipment, it's time to move on to the actual process of making bread. There are a few crucial techniques involved, none of which are complicated, but they are important if you want to get a good result. In the following pages are the various stages involved, ordered as if you were following a recipe.

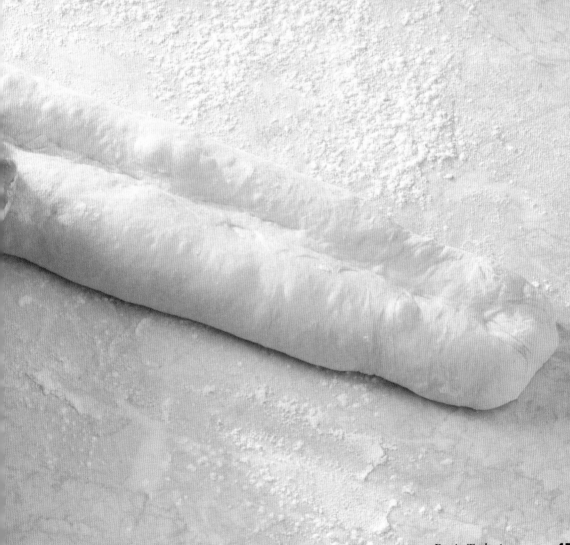

1. Preparing Leaveners

All yeast requires some moisture to help it begin to work. Fresh and active dry yeasts are mixed with liquid before adding to dry ingredients, whereas instant dry yeast is mixed into the dry ingredients before the liquid is added to form the dough. Water is the most common ingredient with which to start your yeast, but you will need to be mindful of the temperature of the water.

If you are using a thermometer, the ideal temperature is between 86°F–98.6°F (30°C–37°C). Without a thermometer, mix two-thirds cold water with one-third boiling water to make a lukewarm temperature that you can comfortably touch. If the liquid is too hot, it will destroy the yeast; too cold, and the yeast will not activate properly.

For fresh yeast: Crumble it into a glass bowl and add lukewarm liquid according to your recipe. Using a wooden spoon, mix the yeast until it dissolves into the water. It is then ready to use.

For active dry yeast: Measure the stated amount of lukewarm liquid into a glass cup, sprinkle it over the active dry yeast, then stir with a wooden spoon to thoroughly dissolve. Active dry yeast takes a bit longer to dissolve than fresh yeast.

For instant dry yeast: Measure the flour and salt stated in the recipe into a glass bowl, mix, then sprinkle over the yeast. Mix it into the flour before adding the lukewarm liquid, otherwise the yeast will not activate properly.

Making and Replenishing a Sourdough Starter

You do need to make some advance preparations if you are planning to use a starter to make your bread. Depending on the recipe you are following, they can take anywhere from a few hours to several days to prepare and ferment, but the ingredients are always the same—flour, water, and usually yeast—although some recipes don't use any yeast.

To store a starter: If you are not ready to use the starter straight away, transfer it to a sterile, sealable glass or noncorrosive jar. Store in the refrigerator for up to two weeks. Let it stand at room temperature for at least 30 minutes before using. Once established, the starter can be kept indefinitely if stored and used correctly. Every time you use some of the starter, you simply replace the flour and water so that you're ready to go again the next time. If you don't use any for two weeks, you need to freshen up and replenish the starter as if you had used some for a recipe.

To replenish a starter: If your recipe uses 10 oz. (300g) starter, you need to replace the amount taken out with 5 oz. (150g) flour and 5 fl. oz. (150mL) water. Carefully blend the old and the new ingredients together, and leave to ferment as before for 24 hours, then store

Sourdough Starter

Here is a starter recipe you can use in relation to specific recipes in this book:

1. Prepare ½ oz. (15g) fresh yeast or 2 tsp. active dry yeast with 3½ fl. oz. (100mL) lukewarm water. Refer to the yeast instructions on the opposite page.

2. Put 9 oz. (250g) white bread flour (or use rice flour for a gluten-free starter) into a very large clean glass bowl, and stir in the prepared yeast. The mixture will bubble and rise quite a lot.

3. Gradually stir in a further 7 fl. oz. (200mL) lukewarm water. Mix well with a wooden spoon to make a smooth, thick batter. If you want to use instant dry yeast, simply stir ¼ oz. (7g) sachet into the flour before adding any water.

Note: This quantity will make enough starter for you to make one loaf with enough left over to replenish it again. If you plan on making more than one loaf at a time, double the quantities above.

4. Cover the bowl with a clean tea towel or piece of cheesecloth (muslin).

5. Keep the mixture at room temperature, ideally more cool than warm, out of direct sunlight. Leave undisturbed for 3 to 5 days. The batter is ready to use when it begins to froth and has a fresh, pleasant, sour aroma.

6. Follow the recipe instructions for using the starter.

in the refrigerator until required again. This should be an ongoing process, enabling you to make a sourdough loaf whenever you want.

2. Mixing

This is the stage where all your ingredients meet each other for the first time. There will be subtle variations between recipes, but in general, this is the route to follow:

Once your yeasty liquid or starter is added to the center of the flour, begin mixing in a little of the flour to start making the dough.

i. If using fresh or active dry yeast, put the flour and salt in a large glass, porcelain, or plastic bowl. If you are making flavored breads (or doughs with additions), your recipe may state that other ingredients are added at this stage too. Make a well in the center using a wooden spoon. If you are using instant dry yeast, make a well in the center of the combined dry flour and yeast.

ii. Pour the yeasty liquid or starter in the center of the well, and gently mix into a little of the flour.

At this stage, some recipes require that the mixture is left to form a soft paste using some of the flour from the bowl. This is called a sponge, and it gives the loaf a lighter crumb and less-yeasty flavor. The mixture is then covered with a clean tea towel or cheesecloth (muslin) and left in a warm place for a specified time to expand. Once the sponge has risen, continue with the method below.

iii. Gradually pour and mix in the remaining quantity of liquid, carefully stirring in the dry ingredients from the outside of the bowl. As you add the liquid, you will notice the consistency of the mixture changing as the ingredients combine. Don't add all the liquid in one go, as it will be more difficult to obtain an even blend, and you may end up not needing all the stated amount of liquid. Variations in manufacturing processes and in wheat and flour quality can affect the amount of liquid necessary to achieve the desired dough texture.

Make sure to carefully stir in the dry ingredients from the outside of the bowl as you mix in the remaining yeasty liquid. The dough should form into a ball in the bowl.

iv. Only continue to add liquid until the mixed dough forms a softish, ball-like mixture in the bowl. If it is still too dry after you have added all the specified liquid, add a little more liquid, teaspoon by teaspoon.

Fold in the edges during kneading.

3. Kneading

This stage of breadmaking is where you establish the basic structure of the mixture. By kneading, you distribute the yeast throughout the dough so that it can start working and producing the gas that causes the bread to rise. At the same time, you are helping to form the gluten, which makes a framework and holds the risen dough in place during baking.

i. Only very lightly dust a clean, dry work surface with the same type of flour you are using in the recipe. Turn the prepared, well-mixed bowl contents onto the surface, and bring the dough together by continually folding the edges into the center until it becomes smoother and easier to work with. At the beginning of kneading, the dough will be slightly sticky and raggedy in texture. If you find the mixture very sticky, add a little flour, but always use extra flour sparingly to avoid making the dough too dry.

ii. Using the heel of one hand, push the dough from the middle, away from you. Roll up the top edge of the dough back toward you. Using the other hand, turn the dough slightly, so that you are gradually pushing and rolling the dough round in a circle. Make sure you keep rotating in one direction only to help form an even texture.

Using the heel of the hand to push dough is most effective.

The dough should stretch as thin as blown bubble gum without breaking, if it is properly kneaded.

iii.Keep these actions going for about 10 minutes or until the dough feels smooth, firm, elastic, and springy to the touch. It can be quite difficult to judge when the dough is sufficiently kneaded, so try the following test: Take a small piece of the dough, and stretch it very, very thinly—as thin as blown bubble gum. If the dough is properly kneaded, it should stretch without breaking.

If the dough doesn't stretch easily and tears, carry on kneading the dough a bit more. This test is more difficult with whole wheat and grain doughs because of the fiber in the dough, and in enriched doughs where the fat coats the flour and affects its flexibility. However, it is still a reliable means to see how far you have come in preparing the dough.

Note: Toward the end of kneading your mixture is the perfect time to add any flavorings you want to use, such as pieces of cheese, chocolate, dried fruits, etc. Adding them at this stage will mean they get properly incorporated without being overprocessed.

iv. Once the dough has been kneaded, press the top a little with your finger, and you will see that it springs back almost immediately. Remember this action, as this is a good benchmark indicator for later when your bread has been left to rise.

v. When you have achieved the desired texture, form the dough into a smooth ball, ready for the next stage.

4. Proving, Knocking Back, and Resting

Prove the dough by placing it in a large bowl, either lightly floured or oiled, and cover with a cheesecloth.

Proving is the term used for leaving the bread dough to rise. Some recipes will call for the bread to rise and others for it to prove. This is a part of the breadmaking process that isn't an exact science. Outside factors will affect the rate your dough rises. Warmth and increased humidity will speed up the dough rise, while a cold environment will slow things down. The type of the flour and whether you have used a starter can also have an effect. When you have made a few loaves, the rising time of the dough will become second nature, but for the first time, it can be difficult to gauge. You should aim for a slow, steady rising process, without being tempted to speed things up.

i. Place the kneaded dough in a large, lightly floured or oiled glass, porcelain, or plastic bowl. The bowl needs to be big enough to allow room for the dough to double in size. Cover the bowl with a clean tea towel or cheesecloth (muslin), and leave to rise at cool room temperature, away from drafts; a cool temperature is fine, but very cold will mean that the yeast will take a long time to get going. In ideal conditions, around 64°F (18°C), the dough should take between 1½ and 2 hours to double in size.

Whole wheat flour and enriched doughs take longer. The slower the dough takes to rise, the more flavor and texture the loaf will have. If you have limited time or your room is exceptionally warm or cold, you can put the dough in the refrigerator for at least 8 hours, where it will rise slowly and steadily. Just cover the bowl with another bowl, making sure the bowls are big enough to allow the dough to expand without being restricted and put in the refrigerator. Before using, refrigerated dough will need to stand for about two hours at room temperature before proceeding to the next stage.

ii. To test that the dough has risen properly, gently press it with your finger. If the indent springs back gradually, then the dough has properly risen; if the indent springs back quickly, then it needs to be left longer. If you've left the dough too long, the indent won't spring back at all, and the dough is overrisen (see Troubleshooting on page 66).

Deflate the dough by pushing your knuckles into the dough, before turning it out on to a lightly floured surface.

iii. Once the dough is risen satisfactorily, push your knuckles into the dough to deflate it, and turn it out onto a lightly floured surface.

iv. Form the dough into a ball by cupping it in your hands and gently turning it on the work surface. As you turn the dough, gently press your hands down the sides of the dough to smooth the sides and then tuck edges underneath. Keep turning and tucking until the dough forms a ball shape. Let the dough rest for five minutes on the work surface before you shape it.

Proving Dough at High Altitude

Rising times are faster at high altitudes due to changes in air pressure. Try letting the dough prove an extra time by deflating the dough with your knuckles twice before shaping and proving before baking. See extra notes on high-altitude breadmaking in the Baking section.

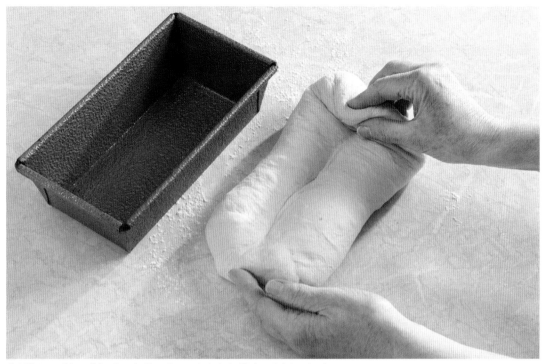

Fold in two sides of the dough, then the ends to help fit dough into a loaf pan.

5. Shaping

There are lots of ways you can shape the dough ready for baking. Here are some of the basic shapes explained. You will also find instructions for shaping some doughs in the instructions of individual recipes. Shaping is an important part of breadmaking, as it helps the structure and texture of the finished loaf. Sprinkle the work surface lightly with the flour you used to make the dough. Handle the dough with care—over-shaping and heavy-handedness will cause the dough to tighten and feel hard; if this happens, let it rest for a few minutes and then proceed gently.

Pan-Baked Loaf—Keeping the dough in a round shape, flatten it gently with the palm of your hand to remove any large air pockets. Roll or press the dough, keeping an even thickness to a size that is 2" (5cm) larger than the size of your loaf pan all around. Fold two sides of the dough toward the center and gently press down. Fold in the ends, and carefully lift and turn the dough over. Make sure it will fit the pan before lowering it, seam-side down, into the pan.

Baguette or Similar Long Loaf—Keeping the dough in a round shape, flatten it gently with the palm of your hand to remove any large air pockets. Fold one side of the dough into the center and fold the other side, overlapping on top. Press gently to seal, then roll gently back and forth to a length that will fit well within your prepared baking tray or to the measurements given in your recipe. Make a deep indent with your thumbs down the center of the roll, fold in the ends, pinch together to seal, and roll again to smooth. Transfer to the baking tray, seam side down.

Pinch the dough together for a round shape.

Smooth out the dough until it's round.

Round—Put the risen dough ball on the work surface and place your hands around the outside. Push your fingers into the base of the dough, tucking the dough into the center of the ball. Turn the dough in your hands and keep tucking the sides underneath until the dough becomes smooth and rounded. Turn the dough over and pinch the seams together—this will be the bottom of the loaf.

Turn the dough back over and cup it in your hands, rotating it and smoothing it, until you are satisfied with the shape. Transfer it to your baking tray. Note: This rounded dough can also be cooked in a large round pan if preferred. The baked loaf will be straight sided with a large domed top.

Oval—Follow the instructions to make a round loaf. Once you have formed the dough correctly, gently press either side of the center with flat, stretched fingers. Gently roll the dough backward and forward, applying even pressure, until the dough becomes sufficiently tapered at the ends. Transfer to a baking sheet.

The start of a braid.

Fold left over center, then right over center.

Braid (Plait) and Twists—For a braid, form three pieces of dough into equal-length sausage shapes by rolling smoothly. Line up the lengths of dough running toward you and pinch them together at the top. Starting with the left piece, fold it over the center piece, then fold the right piece over the piece in the center. Continue folding the dough pieces over each other in this manner until you reach the end, press the pieces together at the end, and tuck both ends underneath.

A simplified version of the braid is a twist, which can be achieved using two long pieces of dough wound simply together and pinched at either end to seal.

Rolls—Roll pieces of dough about the size of a tangerine into small rounds, and press down to get rid of any air bubbles. Cup the dough in your hand and roll it on the floured surface until it forms a smooth, round roll. Note: To achieve uniform rolls, weigh the dough first, then divide into equal portions before shaping.

Rolling Dough—Often it is easier to roll dough for flatter loaves, like focaccia, on an unfloured work surface. This is so that the dough sticks slightly and stretches into shape when pressed or rolled with a rolling pin. If there is too much flour on the surface, you'll find that the dough simply shrinks back after each roll. Keep turning the dough when rolling and use a palette knife to slide under the dough if it sticks too much.

6. Second Proving

Once your loaf or rolls have been shaped and either put in a baking pan or on a baking tray, the shaped dough needs to rest and rise again before baking. This final rising before baking is traditionally referred to as proving. However, in many sources, the word "proving" is interchanged with the word "rising," and it has come to mean the same thing.

This final rising of the bread dough is best done in a warm, draft-free place. If stated in your recipe, cover the loaf pan or trays of rolls with a wide sheet of lightly oiled, greaseproof paper and some cheesecloth (muslin). Drape the layers loosely to allow the dough to rise unhindered underneath.

You should aim to leave the dough until it has doubled in size and feels spongy to the touch and any indents gradually spring back. This usually takes between 30 minutes and 1 hour unless otherwise stated in the recipe. If in doubt, it is better to slightly underprove the dough, because if it proves for too long, it will lose structure and deflate in the oven.

After the second proving, your shaped dough is now ready for the oven. Some bread needs to be cut before baking to

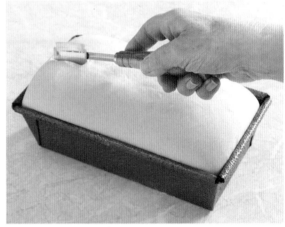

Slashing the top of the bread encourages steam to release during cooking.

encourage a release of steam during cooking and to assist the bread to rise without cracking or bulging. Use a lame; a sharp, thin-bladed knife; or even a pair of kitchen scissors to snip into the dough at intervals. Make the slashes in the dough about ½" (1cm) deep.

Slashing down the middle, crisscross cutting, and diagonal slashes are all common patterning for loaves and rolls. If you are artistic or want to experiment, you can create very attractive patterns on the top of larger loaves and make up unique designs.

7. Glazes and Finishes

Most glazes and toppings are added to the dough once it has proved. Use a soft pastry brush or one with silicone strands to avoid damaging the dough surface. Apply thinly and evenly and make sure you brush right to the edges for an even finish.

There is plenty of choice when it comes to embellishing proved dough. These finishing touches can add extra flavor, color, and texture. Here are a few things you might like to try:

Egg Wash—The most traditional, golden, shiny finish consists of a beaten egg. Simply brush over sweet and savory dough before baking. For an extra-rich brown glaze, reapply the glaze halfway through baking. For a less-golden but glossy glaze, use egg whites only with water. For a rich crust, blend one egg yolk with 1 Tbsp. water.

Make sure to brush the top and edges for an even finish.

Milk or Plant Milk—Brush over the dough for a golden crust on sweet and savory breads.

Melted Butter, Plant Butter, and Vegetable Oil—Brush over sweet or savory loaves to give soft golden crust and extra-rich flavor.

Vegan Glaze—Make a thin, smooth paste from 1 Tbsp. soya flour and 4 tsp. plant-based milk or water. Brush over the surface. This will give a matte, rich, golden color and chewy crust to sweet or savory breads.

Water—Brushing water onto a proved loaf or spraying with a light mister just before baking will give a crisp, golden crust. This technique is used in preparing French baguettes (page 93).

Flour—Simply dust a little flour over the top of the proved dough before baking. Use a small fine sieve for best results. This will give a softer crust to a baked sweet or savory loaf.

Honey, Maple Syrup, or Glacé Icing—For a sticky-sweet finish, brush runny honey or maple syrup over bread as soon as it comes out of the oven. Once the bread has cooled, dust with powdered sugar, or drizzle sweet loaves or buns with a simple icing made from powdered sugar and water or fruit juice.

As well as brushing the dough with a glaze, you may want to add a topping. The glaze will act as an adhesive to enable you to keep the topping in place during baking. Here are some embellishments you may like to try:

For savory breads: small seeds; finely chopped or flaked nuts; rolled oats; bran flakes; cracked wheat; cornmeal; grated cheese; finely shredded, cooked onion; coarse salt; freshly ground black pepper; lightly cracked spice seeds (fennel, caraway, cumin, and cilantro); a little chili powder; plain or smoked paprika; or tiny sprigs of fresh herbs.

For sweet breads: poppy seeds; rolled oats; superfine or coarse sugars like Demerara; crushed sugar lumps; or ground spices like cinnamon, ginger, and finely crushed cardamom seeds.

8. Baking

Last but by no means least, the final stage of breadmaking. Always preheat the oven to the temperature given in the recipe unless otherwise directed. Most bread is cooked in a hot oven, about 425°F (220°C/200°C fan oven). Bread requires an even cooking temperature, but all ovens cook differently, and temperatures may vary. If in any doubt about your oven's temperature regulation, use a thermometer inside your oven to make sure.

Place bread on the middle shelf of the oven, and make sure that you either arrange the shelf above a good distance away from the top of the loaf or take it out altogether. If your oven has a "hot spot," make sure you turn your bread around halfway through cooking time. Cooking times vary depending on the recipe and the size of your loaf. Some recipes call for extra moisture or steam during baking, and this can be achieved by placing a tray of water in the bottom of the oven—take care when opening the oven door as the steam will be scorching.

Baking Adjustments for High Altitudes

The recipes and baking times in this book are averages; results may vary somewhat depending on the altitude. Due to changes in air pressure, the higher the altitude, the less time it takes to bake things. As a general guideline, if the altitude is 3,000 feet (914m) or higher, decrease baking time between 5 and 8 minutes per 30 minutes of total baking time; adjust the oven temperature accordingly, increasing by 15°F–25°F (10°C–20°C). You might also try reducing the yeast quantity of the recipe by one-quarter, and adding a little extra liquid to help improve the moisture level. Achieving a perfect loaf at high altitudes may require some experimentation, so record your results for your own reference.

How Do You Know When Your Bread is Cooked?

A perfectly cooked loaf should be well risen and have a light-to-golden brown crust that is firm but not hard in texture. Unlike a cake mixture, which can be tested with a skewer or toothpick for doneness, the crust on a loaf of bread makes it impossible to find out whether the mixture underneath is cooked through. The best means of testing if your loaf is cooked properly is to cover your hand with a clean cloth or tea towel, and carefully turn the bread out onto your clothed hand. Tap the underside of the loaf gently with your fingers; it should sound hollow when it is properly cooked.

Immediately turn your cooked loaf on to a wire rack. Allow the loaf to cool completely by transferring it onto a wire rack; transfer rolls onto a rack using a spatula. Cooling your bread in this way allows steam to escape quickly from the depths of the loaf without getting trapped and causing the bread to go soggy.

Always cool your bread loaf on a wire rack to allow steam to escape from the loaf without getting trapped and causing soggy bread.

Cut the perfect bread slice by using a steady sawing motion across and through the top crust, and then cutting straight down the loaf.

9. The Perfect Slice

For maximum freshness, always cut your bread just before serving, as it dries out quickly and becomes stale. Bread doesn't have to be completely cool before you cut it, but if too hot, the knife will drag the crumb textures together and make the texture doughy—you will also not benefit from the flavor if the bread is too hot when you eat it.

Baguettes and long loaves are usually cut into chunky slices. While other types of loaf are more thinly sliced, though not too thin, bread cut in thicker slices will enable you to enjoy the full flavor of your freshly baked loaf. Bread of all types is traditionally served in wicker or cane ware. This natural fiber helps keep the bread fresh and will tolerate heat if you're serving the bread warm.

To cut the perfect slice, sit the loaf on a clean wooden board (used only for bread). Use a sharp, serrated bread knife. Cut with a steady sawing action across the top of the crust and continue straight down the loaf, sawing all the time to prevent spoiling the crumb—if you press down on a loaf, you will risk squishing the crumbs together, causing a doughy texture.

10. Reheating

If you've baked bread earlier in the day and want to serve it warm, a very easy "green" and economical way is to simply put cooked rolls or flatbreads in a slow-cooker dish. Cover with the lid, switch on to the high setting, and leave for about 20 minutes or so to warm through.

To use more conventional means, arrange your bread on a baking tray, spray lightly with water, and place uncovered in a preheated oven at 400°F (200°C/180°C fan oven). Crusty loaves will take about 5 minutes to warm up and crisp. Rolls need only 2–3 minutes. You can also use a multicooker or air fryer to reheat in the same way as well. Pita and naan breads can be reheated in a toaster if they fit, in a heated dry frying pan, or by placing under a hot grill for 1–2 minutes on each side—drizzle them or spray lightly with water before heating.

11. Storing And Freezing

How long bread stays fresh can depend on a few factors. Some recipes will state that a certain loaf is best eaten on the day of baking—these tend to be small or thin, plainer breads, such as white bread rolls, some flat breads, and baguettes. Larger, thicker loaves will usually last a few days if stored correctly. Loaves enriched with fat or oil are usually good keepers, as are the more rustic breads made with a starter. Gluten-free and yeast-free breads (soda bread)

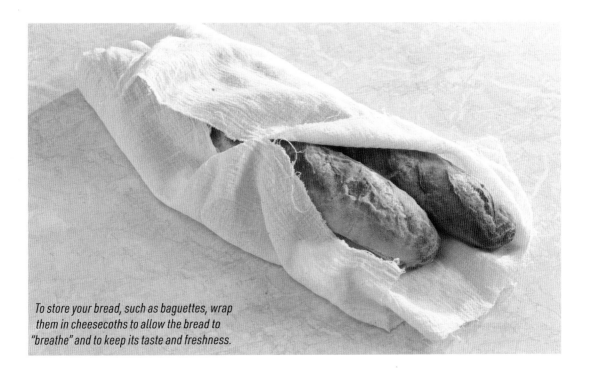

To store your bread, such as baguettes, wrap them in cheesecoths to allow the bread to "breathe" and to keep its taste and freshness.

tend to dry out quite quickly once a slice has been taken off. Below are a few tips to help you store your bread:

- **Bread must be completely cold before storing.** Any warmth in the loaf will speed up mold growth or make the bread become stale quickly.

- **Keep bread at room temperature,** away from direct sunlight, in a cool and dry place.

- **Keep the crusty end of the loaf** after cutting, and use as a natural seal for the end of the loaf. Other ways of achieving this is to wrap the end in greaseproof paper and aluminum foil, but make sure you only cover the end; avoid wrapping the whole loaf in paper and foil as this will make the loaf "sweat" and lose its crustiness and texture. Alternatively, stand the loaf, cut side down on a bread board. If you have a clean paper bag, you could wrap this around the bread or drape with cheesecloth (muslin) or a clean tea towel. Plastic will make the bread soft.

- **Bread needs to "breathe"** for better keeping. You will find cloth bags specifically designed for wrapping around a loaf, but you could try a clean tea towel or piece of cheesecloth (muslin). A note from personal experience: Avoid using a tea towel that has been freshly washed in particularly fragrant laundry soap, otherwise you will end up with very strange-tasting bread! You may prefer to store your wrapped bread away from the work surface; an earthenware crock or wooden, wicker, or metal bread bin are suitable. Make sure they don't seal completely tight—air needs to circulate. You can use a plastic container, but make sure you put some holes in the top and sides.

- **Avoid putting bread in the refrigerator** as this makes it dehydrate quickly and become stale. It is also likely to absorb aromas from other foods and become tainted.

Freezing and Defrosting

For long-term storage, freezing is the obvious solution. You can freeze cooked bread as well as bread dough.

For baked bread: After thoroughly cooling baked bread, slice it beforehand for convenience or leave it whole. Make sure the bread is wrapped and well-sealed, use heavy-duty aluminum foil, and then put in a freezer bag or container. Seal well and keep for up to three months. Rolls, thin breads, gluten-free breads, and nonyeasted breads are best frozen as soon as they are cool on the day of baking; they can be wrapped and frozen like the larger loaves. Remember to date and label your breads.

To defrost baked bread: Cooked bread is best defrosted slowly. It is quite an art to "quick defrost" in the microwave oven and is often a bit hit or miss. Frozen slices can be cooked directly on the frozen bread setting in a toaster, but other than that, a slow thaw is best. Keep your frozen bread in the freezer wrappings, and let it stand at room temperature for about 3 hours or in the refrigerator for up to 10 hours until it has thawed. When thawed in this way, it will be difficult to distinguish it from freshly baked, and it should retain moistness without drying out. If you want to crisp up the crust, place the thawed loaf in a low or warm oven for 5–10 minutes—no longer, otherwise you will have hot bread! Bread can only be reheated once to crisp it up, after which time it will simply dry out and become stale.

For dough: Once the dough is mixed and kneaded, form it into a neat ball shape. Oil the inside of a clean freezer bag or container and put the dough inside. The container needs to be big enough to allow the dough to expand a little; it will take a while for the yeast to become inactive in the freezer. Expel all the air from the bag, leaving a little room for the dough to expand slightly as it freezes, then seal well. Date, label, and freeze for up to three months.

To defrost dough: Carefully remove the dough from the freezer. While frozen, place in a large oiled glass, porcelain, or plastic bowl—the bowl needs to be big enough to allow sufficient room for the dough to rise. Cover with a bowl, place in the fridge and leave for up to 24 hours or until doubled in size. Remove from the fridge and stand at room temperature for 2 hours to thoroughly take the chill off, then you can deflate, rest, shape, second prove, and bake your dough as stated in your recipe.

Cut freshly baked and cooled bread into slices before freezing for extra convenience.

Many issues can arise when making bread. Learn the common pitfalls and solutions so you can avoid the dreaded burnt bread.

Troubleshooting

Even if you follow a recipe in detail, sometimes you will encounter problems with your baking. Here are some of the most-common problems that you might come across.

Raw Dough Problems

Dry Dough During Mixing—When you first mix the yeasty liquid into the flour and gradually add the remaining liquid, you may end up with a very firm mixture that has no stickiness to it. This is because it is virtually impossible to state the exact quantity of liquid required to make a perfectly combined mixture—different types of flour and different manufacturers' flours absorb liquid at different rates. Simply add more liquid, one teaspoon at a time, mixing it in between each, until you have mixed the dough properly together.

Dry Dough During Kneading—When you come to knead the dough, you may find it too stiff and hard to manipulate. Use a water spray to add liquid in very small amounts so that the dough absorbs the extra moisture without becoming sticky. You can also achieve this by wetting your hands with water to knead the dough. Keep wetting them until you have the right textured dough.

Wet Dough—If you turn your dough on to the work surface and it seems excessively wet or the dough sticks to your fingers as you work it, dust the dough lightly with the flour used in your recipe. Keep kneading in sufficient extra flour in very small dustings until the dough feels smooth and comes away from your fingers as you knead. Keep in mind that the more flour you add at this stage, the drier the crumb will be in the baked loaf.

Dough Doesn't Rise—There could be a few reasons why this happens:

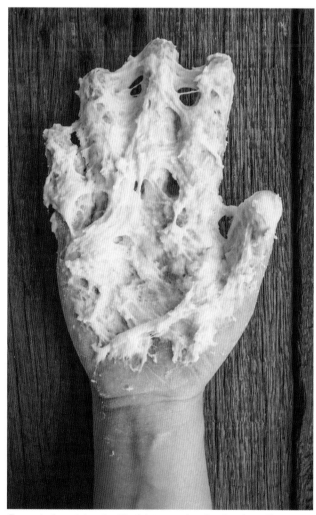

Excessively wet dough will stick to your hands when kneading.

- The yeast may not be as fresh as you thought. Check the expiry date and how it's been stored; if this is the cause, you will have to discard the mixture and start a fresh batch.
- The liquid used was either too hot or too cold. Yeast has been destroyed or not given the right conditions to get going. If you have got the liquid temperature incorrect, it is better to start again.
- The dough is too dry and stiff. Lack of moisture will mean the yeast doesn't work properly, and the gluten doesn't develop in the kneading process—refer to information given for "Dry Dough."
- If after the first or second proving period, the dough hasn't risen, this may be because the conditions were too cold. Put the mixture somewhere warmer and see if this sets off the rise.
- Too much salt added to the mixture will inhibit the yeast from working. Measure salt carefully. If you are concerned you've added too much salt, taste a small piece of dough. It is difficult to correct too much salt, and it is better to start again.

Dough is Overproved—If the dough is very puffed up and the finger test on the risen dough makes an imprint that doesn't spring back, then it has been left too long. The dough will usually deflate and there will be a strong smell of fermenting yeast. You can try to reclaim the dough by kneading it very briefly, shaping the dough, and leaving it for a short proving period before baking. Remember that it is better to leave the dough to prove in a cool temperature for a slow, steady rise—too warm, and the yeast will set to work too quickly and not achieve the correct result.

Another factor to consider here is the use of salt. Perhaps you forgot to add any? Salt controls yeast activity and acts as a "brake." If you haven't added any, there will be a chance that the yeast has become overactive, and the dough will expand more than it should. Taste a little piece of the dough if you are unsure. Most recipes call for salt to be about 2% of the weight of the flour.

Shaped Bread is Overproved—This happens when you leave your shaped bread too long on its second rise before baking. You will see that the loaf has either risen too much in its pan, or free-standing loaves or rolls will look puffy and misshapen. If you were to go on to bake the bread in this state, it will more than likely collapse in the oven. You can try and reclaim the dough as mentioned above, but this time, only leave it to prove for a very short time, just until you can see it starting to rise again. Then bake as directed.

Too much flour used during shaping will cause the dough to dry out on top and crack during baking.

Baked Bread Problems

Lack of Rise—Refer to information given for "Dry Dough." Refer to notes on insufficient kneading and lack of gluten development; and insufficient rising time—yeast hasn't had chance to develop properly. Try the test under "Proving, Knocking Back, and Resting."

Bread has Collapsed—Refer to notes on "Dough is Overproved." If the loaf collapses during the initial cooking period, it is because the extra heat from the oven has caused the dough to overprove. If there is too much dough for the pan, the dough will expand too much; at the extreme, it will run down the side of the pan and the loaf will not form a domed top. Make sure you use the correct amount of dough for your pan.

Uneven Shape—Either the pan is the wrong size, or the dough hasn't been properly kneaded. Always use the stated size of pan in the recipe you are following. Make sure you thoroughly knead the bread dough to allow the gluten to form a proper structure in the dough. Take care to seal the ends of loaves for free-form shapes to achieve a neat finish. Slashing the top with a lame or small sharp knife will also help a loaf rise more evenly by releasing pockets of trapped gas more quickly before the structure of the loaf bakes. Cut to about ½" (1cm) deep for best results.

Cracks on the Outside of the Loaf

Cracked Top—Too much flour used during shaping causes the dough to dry out on top. Try to use a minimal amount of flour when kneading and preparing the dough. Also, make sure you follow the directions for shaping the dough to make a smooth, crease-free ball of dough from which to shape your rolls or loaf. Insufficient slashing on top of the loaf or no slashing at all can also cause the crust to crack unevenly—see "Uneven Shape."

Cracked Sides—Insufficient proving can cause this to happen. When the bread goes into the oven, it gets a sudden burst of heat and causes the yeast to put on a real spurt of action, making the structure split. Follow the test for judging the correct amount of time to prove your dough. See also "Uneven Shape."

The Crust

Most of us know that the brown crust forms on bread due to caramelization, but a lesser-known process called the Maillard reaction is taking place as well. Named after the French scientist who discovered it, this happens when a specific food is subjected to heat either in the oven, under the grill, or in a frying pan. Certain proteins on the surface of the food combine with carbohydrates in the flour to make the surface turn brown and give the familiar flavor of "toast" that we associate with a good bread crust. The Maillard reaction also occurs on the surface of cooked meat, roasted coffee, and cocoa beans, and in the brewing of dark beers.

Here are a few problems that may occur with the bread's crust:

The Crust is Pale—To obtain a well-formed crust on a loaf, you need to make sure your oven is hot enough. If in doubt, check with a special oven thermometer placed inside the oven. Other factors that inhibit the formation of the crust can be insufficient sugar in the dough, lack of moisture, and the overproving in a warm place. If you are concerned about the dough drying out during rising or proving, try covering it with a clean, damp tea towel to keep the conditions moist. You can then occasionally spray the towel lightly with water if necessary.

The Crust is Too Dark—Your oven may be too hot, or you've cooked the bread for too long. If in doubt, check with a special oven thermometer placed inside the oven. You can shield a loaf that's browning too quickly with a piece of aluminum foil. It is important to cook bread long enough, otherwise the middle will be doughy and indigestible. If your bread is an enriched dough, take care to measure the sugar correctly, as this too can cause a very dark crust.

Soggy or Wet Crust—This occurs when the bread has been allowed to cool in the pan. Steam gets trapped and goes back into the loaf as moisture, causing the crust to become soft. Always turn your loaves out on to a wire rack as soon as they are baked. Transfer free-standing loaves and rolls to a wire rack as soon as they come out of the oven.

Baked Crust Separates from Bread—When you cut into your bread for the first time, you may encounter a pocket of air running down the length of the loaf between the crust and the rest of the bread. This is usually caused when the shaped bread has been left a bit too long to prove in too dry conditions. This will cause the outside of the loaf to form a crusty edge. The weaker, overrisen dough inside will begin to collapse back away from it because the yeast has become exhausted. When the bread is baked in this condition, the top crust forms a thicker crusty edge than normal because it has set in place; the dough underneath is not able to rise sufficiently to reach it, and so an air pocket forms between the rest of the dough and the crust. Make sure you prove you bread in the right conditions.

Make sure to prove your bread in the right conditions to avoid uneven structures in your loaves after baking.

Brush glaze lightly and thinly on the top of the bread, and then brush around the edge to avoid drip marks.

Crust is Too Thick—Often found in a loaf when a crust separates from the rest of the bread and the final rise has been overdone. It can also occur in an enriched bread dough if there isn't sufficient sugar to brown off the very top crust.

Uneven Finish on Top Crust—Glaze has been applied too thickly or unevenly. To avoid "drip" marks on the crust, make sure you brush glazes lightly and thinly all over the top and then brush around the edge to mop up any excess glaze.

Eating undercooked bread is not recommended. It is unpleasant and potentially dangerous if it contains ingredients like eggs. Always check your bread is cooked at the correct temperature by using an oven thermometer, and it should sound hollow when tapped underneath .

Bread Texture Problems

Sour Flavor and Smell—Commonly a sour flavor will occur if the dough has been overrisen or has risen too quickly in too high a temperature; there will probably be a too-yeasty smell as well. If you don't cook your bread long enough, the yeast will not be destroyed by sufficient heat, and the aroma and flavor will linger in the bread, and it will also have a doughy texture. As well as tasting unpleasant, eating undercooked dough is not recommended. Raw flours are difficult to digest, and other ingredients like undercooked egg may cause food poisoning if also contained in the loaf. It is best discarded.

Heavy and "Gummy"—The bread has been baked at too high a temperature. If in doubt about your oven thermostat, use an oven thermometer. If the crust browns too early, the loaf can't expand to its maximum volume; the texture of the bread is unable to form correctly and remains closed, crumbed, and underrisen. If you haven't cooked the bread for long enough, while the outside looks done, the inner crumb will be gummy and lacking in flavor. Always tap the base of the loaf for a hollow sound to test for doneness. Heavy bread is best discarded.

Too Crumbly and Dry—This is usually caused by using a grade of flour that doesn't contain enough protein. For best results, always use the best-quality flour you can afford.

Large air holes—While you want your bread to have some holes, large pockets of air are unsatisfactory unless appropriate for the recipe, such as ciabatta. This is often caused by poor kneading when the yeast is badly distributed in the dough. During shaping, make sure you press the dough to squeeze out large pockets of trapped air. Also, overproving can cause air pockets to form as the yeast becomes overactive.

Press and squeeze the dough during kneading to release any unwanted large pockets of trapped air before shaping.

White Floury Patches are Present in Cooked Loaf—This may happen when you use extra flour during kneading or shaping. The flour gets into the dough but doesn't get thoroughly mixed in, forming pockets of raw flour in the dough. Try to refrain from adding extra during the last stages of kneading, and if you do, keep it as light a dusting as possible. Use a small fine sieve for minimal dusting.

Mold on bread is often the result of it being kept in a warm environment or in a plastic bag, where it becomes infected by microbes.

Mold

Bread contains much less moisture than many foods; it dries out quickly and can become infected by microbes that spoil the crumb and crust. If you keep bread in a warm environment or in a plastic bag, this will encourage moisture to form on the bread, which in turn encourages potentially toxic molds to develop. Always discard moldy bread to avoid potentially harmful health risks.

Once you are familiar with the breadmaking process, creating and baking bread dough will become second nature.

Recipes

One of the best kitchen aromas is the smell of freshly baked bread. In the following pages, you will find recipes for delicious breads from around the world. To get you started on your bread-making journey, try the Basic White Bread recipe first. Once you've mastered that, you'll be ready to delve into the exciting world of sourdoughs, baguettes, and heavenly, buttery brioche.

Basic White Bread

A good recipe to get you started. From this one simple loaf, you will be able to make many variations.

Makes: one 2 lb. (900g) loaf

Preparation Time: 35 minutes, plus proving

Cooking Time: 40 minutes

Ingredients

- ¾ oz. (20g) fresh yeast or 2½ tsp. active dry yeast or 2¾ tsp. instant dry yeast
- 13 fl. oz. (375mL) lukewarm water
- 1 lb. 5 oz. (600g) very strong white bread flour, plus extra for dusting
- 2 tsp. salt

Directions

1. Crumble the fresh yeast into a small glass bowl and add 5 fl. oz. (150mL) of the lukewarm water. Using a wooden spoon, mix the yeast until it dissolves into the water. If using active dry yeast, sprinkle the yeast over the same amount of lukewarm water and proceed as for fresh yeast. If using instant dry yeast, simply mix straight into the flour before adding any water.

2. Mix the flour and salt in a large mixing bowl and make a well in the center. Pour the yeasty liquid into the center of the well and gently mix into the flour using a wooden spoon.

3. Gradually pour and mix in the remaining water, carefully stirring in the dry ingredients from the outside of the bowl to form a softish, ball-like mixture in the middle of the bowl.

4. Turn the dough onto a lightly floured work surface and knead until smooth and elastic, for about 10 minutes.

5. Put the dough in a large, lightly floured glass, porcelain, or plastic bowl. The bowl needs to be big enough to allow room for the dough to double in size. Cover the bowl with a clean tea towel or cheesecloth (muslin). Leave it to rise at a coolish room temperature, away from drafts, for about 2 hours or until it has doubled in size.

6. Once the dough has risen satisfactorily, push your knuckles into the dough to deflate it, and turn it out onto a lightly floured surface. Form the dough into a ball, and let it rest for 5 minutes on the work surface before you shape it.

7. Grease a 2 lb. (900g) loaf pan. Shape the dough to fit the pan and place it, seam side down, in the pan. Cover with a large bowl and leave it to prove in a warm place until it has doubled in size.

8. Meanwhile, preheat the oven to 425°F (220°C/200°C fan oven). Remove the bowl covering the loaf. Using a lame or sharp knife, cut a slash down the center of the loaf about ½" (1cm) deep. Dust lightly with a little flour and bake in the center of the oven for about 40 minutes, until golden brown and hollow sounding when tapped underneath. Turn out on to a wire rack to cool.

For a Crusty Finish

Brush the loaf with a beaten egg or vegan glaze (page 59) just before baking.

Basic White Bread Rolls

Makes: 12 bread rolls

1. Follow the recipe above to the end of step 6. Weigh the dough and divide into 12 equal portions.

2. Shape each portion and place on 2 large, lightly floured baking trays. Cover loosely with cheesecloth (muslin), and leave to prove until it has doubled in size. Finishing options: slash with a lame, dust with flour, brush with an egg or vegan glaze, or sprinkle with seeds.

3. Bake in a preheated oven as in step 8 for about 20 minutes, swapping the trays halfway through. Transfer to a wire rack to cool.

Free-Form White Loaf

A variation of white bread that uses standard plain flour mixed with white bread flour to give a softer texture. This dough works best with fresh yeast; it's shaped by hand and baked, so no pan required!

Makes: one 2 lb. (900g) loaf, approx. 9" (23cm) diameter
Preparation Time: 35 minutes, plus proving
Cooking Time: 35 minutes

Ingredients

- ¾ oz. (20g) fresh yeast
- 12fl. oz. (350mL) lukewarm water
- 14 oz. (400g) white bread flour
- 7 oz. (200g) all-purpose flour
- 2 tsp. salt
- 1 Tbsp. sunflower oil

Directions

1. Crumble the fresh yeast into a small glass bowl and add 5 fl. oz. (150mL) of the lukewarm water. Using a wooden spoon, mix the yeast until it dissolves into the water.

2. Mix the flours and salt in a large mixing bowl and make a well in the center. Pour the yeasty liquid into the center of the well and gently mix into the flour using a wooden spoon.

3. Add the oil. Gradually pour and mix in the remaining water, carefully stirring in the dry ingredients from the outside of the bowl to form a softish, ball-like mixture in the middle of the bowl.

4. Turn the dough onto a lightly floured work surface and knead until smooth and elastic, for about 10 minutes.

5. Put the dough in a large, lightly floured glass, porcelain, or plastic bowl. The bowl needs to be big enough to allow room for the dough to double in size. Cover the bowl with a clean tea towel or cheesecloth (muslin). Leave it to rise at a coolish room temperature, away from drafts, for about 2 hours or until it has doubled in size.

6. Once the dough has risen satisfactorily, push your knuckles into the dough to deflate it and turn it out onto a lightly floured surface. Form the dough into a ball and let it rest for 5 minutes on the work surface before you shape it into a round shape.

7. Carefully transfer the shaped dough to a large, lightly floured baking tray, seam side down. Cover with a large bowl, and set aside to prove in a warm place until it has doubled in size.

8. Meanwhile, preheat the oven to 425°F (220°C/200°C fan oven). Remove the covering from the loaf, and using a lame or sharp knife, cut a crisscross design over the top of the loaf, about ½" (1cm) deep. Brush with cold water and bake in the center of the oven for about 35 minutes, until golden brown and hollow sounding when tapped underneath. Transfer to a wire rack to cool.

Whole Wheat Loaf

I do like to eat healthily, but I have always struggled with very fibrous bread. This is my way of making a nutritious loaf that still feels a bit naughty too!

The method includes making a sponge (page 50), so it is more suitable for using with fresh or active dry yeast.

Makes: one 1 lb. 11 oz. (775g) loaf, approx. 7" (18cm) diameter
Preparation Time: 35 minutes, plus proving
Cooking Time: 35 minutes

Ingredients

- ½ oz. (15g) fresh yeast or 2 tsp. active dry yeast
- 10½ fl. oz. (315mL) lukewarm water
- 10 oz. (300g) whole wheat bread flour, plus extra for dusting
- 7 oz. (200g) white bread flour
- 1½ tsp. salt
- 1 Tbsp. soft light brown sugar

Directions

1. Crumble the fresh yeast into a small glass bowl and add 3½ fl. oz. (100mL) of the lukewarm water. Using a wooden spoon, mix the yeast until it dissolves into the water. If using active dry yeast, sprinkle the yeast over the same amount of lukewarm water and proceed as for fresh yeast.

2. Mix the flours, salt, and sugar in a large mixing bowl and make a well in the center. Pour the yeasty liquid in the center of the well, and gently mix it using a wooden spoon with a little of the flour to form a smooth paste. Cover with a clean tea towel and leave at room temperature for about 20 minutes, until the paste forms a "sponge" and is frothy and bubbling.

3. Gradually pour and mix in the remaining water, carefully stirring in the dry ingredients from the outside of the bowl to form a softish, ball-like mixture in the middle of the bowl.

4. Turn the dough onto a lightly floured work surface and knead until smooth and elastic, for about 10 minutes.

5. Put the dough in a large, lightly floured glass, porcelain, or plastic bowl. The bowl needs to be big enough to allow room for the dough to double in size. Cover the bowl with a clean tea towel or cheesecloth (muslin). Leave it to rise at a coolish room temperature, away from drafts, for about 2 hours or until it has doubled in size.

6. Once the dough has risen satisfactorily, push your knuckles into the dough to deflate it and turn it out onto a lightly floured surface. Form the dough into a ball and let it rest for 5 minutes on the work surface before you shape it.

7. Grease and line a 2½" (6cm) deep, 7" (18cm) diameter, round pan. Shape the dough to fit the pan and place it seam side down. Cover with a large bowl and set aside to prove in a warm place until it has doubled in size.

8. Meanwhile, preheat the oven to 425°F (220°C/200°C fan oven). Remove the covering from the loaf, and using a lame or sharp knife, cut a cross in the top of the loaf about ½" (1cm) deep. Dust lightly with flour and bake in the center of the oven for about 35 minutes, until lightly golden and hollow sounding when tapped underneath. Turn out on to a wire rack to cool.

Whole Wheat Rolls

You can use this dough to make 10 rolls, following the directions for Basic White Bread Rolls (page 80).

Poppy Seed Braid

This dough is made using milk as the liquid and is therefore also known as milk loaf. The crumb is finer and the crust soft and glossy.

Makes: one 1 lb. 11 oz. (775g), approx. 10" (25cm) long plaited loaf

Preparation Time: 40 minutes, plus proving

Cooking Time: 35 minutes

Ingredients

- ½ oz. (15g) fresh yeast or 2 tsp. active dry yeast or ¼ oz. (7g) sachet instant dry yeast
- 10 fl. oz. (300mL) lukewarm 2% milk
- 1 lb. 2 oz. (500g) white bread flour
- 1½ tsp. salt
- 1 egg, beaten, or 2 Tbsp. (30mL) vegan glaze (page 59)
- 2 tsp. poppy seeds

Poppy seeds look great on top of bread, but they also add texture that is a delight to eat.

Directions

1. Crumble the fresh yeast into a small glass bowl and add 3½ fl. oz. (100mL) of the lukewarm milk. Using a wooden spoon, mix the yeast until it dissolves into the milk. If using active dry yeast, sprinkle the yeast over the same amount of lukewarm milk and proceed as for fresh yeast. If using instant dry yeast, simply mix straight into the flour before adding any milk.

2. Mix the flour and salt in a large mixing bowl and make a well in the center. Pour the yeasty milk in the center of the well and gently mix into the flour using a wooden spoon.

3. Gradually pour and mix in the remaining milk, carefully stirring in the dry ingredients from the outside of the bowl to form a softish, ball-like mixture in the middle of the bowl.

4. Turn the dough onto a lightly floured work surface and knead until smooth and elastic, for about 10 minutes.

5. Put the dough in a large, lightly floured glass, porcelain, or plastic bowl. The bowl needs to be big enough to allow room for the dough to double in size. Cover the bowl with a clean tea towel or cheesecloth (muslin). Leave it to rise at a coolish room temperature, away from drafts, for about 2 hours or until it has doubled in size.

6. Once the dough has risen satisfactorily, push your knuckles into the dough to deflate it and turn it out onto a lightly floured surface. Form the dough into a ball and let it rest for 5 minutes on the work surface before you shape it.

7. Divide the dough into 3 equal portions, and roll each into a thick sausage about 12" (30cm) long. Braid the dough.

8. Carefully transfer to a large, lightly floured baking sheet, seam side down. Cover loosely with a large bowl, and set aside to prove in a warm place until it has doubled in size.

9. Meanwhile, preheat the oven to 425°F (220°C/200°C fan oven). Remove the bowl and brush all over with a beaten egg. Sprinkle with poppy seeds and bake in the center of the oven for about 35 minutes, until glossy golden brown and hollow sounding when tapped underneath. Transfer to a wire rack to cool.

Poppy Seed Pan Loaf
Tuck the ends under to fit the length of a lightly greased 2 lb. (900g) loaf pan, then carefully lower into the pan, seam side down. Prove, glaze, seed, and bake as in step 9.

Spelt Bloomer

An interesting, textured whole wheat–style loaf. This ancient grain has a different gluten structure and subsequently produces a denser, cakier crumb. The flour is also quite absorbent, so you may need to add a little more water.

Makes: one 1 lb. 9 oz. (700g) loaf

Preparation Time: 35 minutes, plus proving

Cooking Time: 40 minutes

Ingredients

- ½ oz. (15g) fresh yeast or 2 tsp. active dry yeast or ¼ oz. (7g) sachet instant dry yeast
- 9½ fl. oz. (275mL) lukewarm water
- 1 lb. 2 oz. (500g) whole wheat spelt flour
- 1½ tsp. salt
- 1 Tbsp. maple syrup
- 1 Tbsp. good-quality olive oil

Spelt Rolls

You can use this dough to make 10 rolls, following the directions for Basic White Bread Rolls (page 80). Bake at 400°F (200°C) for about 25 minutes.

Directions

1. Crumble the fresh yeast into a small glass bowl and add 3½ fl. oz. (100mL) of the lukewarm water. Using a wooden spoon, mix the yeast until it dissolves into the water. If using active dry yeast, sprinkle the yeast over the same amount of lukewarm water and proceed as for fresh yeast. If using instant dry yeast, simply mix straight into the flour before adding any water.

2. Mix the flour and salt in a large mixing bowl and make a well in the center. Add the syrup, oil, and yeasty water to the center of the well and gently mix into the flour using a wooden spoon.

3. Gradually pour and mix in the remaining water, carefully stirring in the dry ingredients from the outside of the bowl to form a softish, ball-like mixture in the middle of the bowl.

4. Turn the dough onto a lightly floured work surface and knead until smooth and elastic, for about 10 minutes. If the dough feels quite "tight" or stiff, add a little more water using a water spray until it feels more flexible.

5. Put the dough in a large, lightly floured glass, porcelain, or plastic bowl. The bowl needs to be big enough to allow room for the dough to double in size. Cover the bowl with a clean tea towel or cheesecloth (muslin). Leave it to rise at a coolish room temperature, away from drafts, for about 2 hours or until it has doubled in size.

6. Once the dough has risen satisfactorily, push your knuckles into the dough to deflate it and turn it out onto a lightly floured surface. Form the dough into a ball and let it rest for 5 minutes on the work surface before you shape it.

7. Shape the dough into a long oval shape about 10" (25cm) in length. Carefully transfer to a large, lightly floured baking tray, seam side down. Cover with a bowl and set aside to prove in a warm place until it has doubled in size.

8. Meanwhile, preheat the oven to 400°F (200°C/180°C fan oven). Using a lame or sharp knife, cut diagonal slashes about ½" (1cm) deep, down the length of the dough. Lightly dust with flour and bake in the center of the oven for about 40 minutes, until lightly golden and hollow sounding when tapped underneath. Transfer to a wire rack to cool.

Spelt Pan Loaf

Shape the mixture, and place in a lightly greased 2 lb. (900g) loaf pan, seam side down. Prove and bake as in the directions.

Baguette

A unique style of bread with a crisp, golden crust and deliciously airy, chewy crumb. Traditionally, French stick loaves are baked in perforated, rounded pans that give the familiar baguette shape. Using baking trays will give you a flatter baked loaf. For the best results, use fresh yeast and prove overnight in the fridge.

Makes: two 12 oz. (350g) baguettes

Preparation Time: 45 minutes, plus overnight proving, standing, and additional proving

Cooking Time: 25 minutes

Ingredients

- ½ oz. (15g) fresh yeast
- 12 fl. oz. (350mL) lukewarm water
- 1 lb. 2 oz. (500g) white bread flour, plus extra to dust
- 1½ tsp. salt

Baking on a tray will give baguettes a flatter base.

Directions

1. Crumble the yeast into a small glass bowl and add 5 fl. oz. (150mL) of the lukewarm water. Using a wooden spoon, mix the yeast until it dissolves into the water.

2. Mix the flour and salt in a large mixing bowl and make a well in the center. Pour the yeasty liquid in the center of the well, and gently mix using a wooden spoon with a little of the flour to form a smooth paste. Cover with a clean tea towel and leave it at room temperature for about 20 minutes, until the paste forms a "sponge" and is frothy and bubbling.

3. Gradually pour and mix in the remaining water, carefully stirring in the dry ingredients from the outside of the bowl to form a softish, ball-like mixture in the middle of the bowl.

4. Turn the dough onto a lightly floured work surface and knead until smooth and elastic, for about 10 minutes.

5. Put the dough in a large, lightly oiled glass, porcelain, or plastic bowl. The bowl needs to be big enough to allow room for the dough to double in size. Cover the bowl with another large bowl or domed lid. Leave it to prove slowly overnight in the fridge until it has doubled in size.

6. The next day, remove the dough from the fridge and stand at room temperature for 2 hours to thoroughly take the chill off. Push your knuckles into the dough to deflate it and turn it out onto a lightly floured surface. Form the dough into a ball.

7. Return the dough ball to the bowl, re-cover, and leave to re-prove at coolish room temperature until it has doubled in size. Repeat this deflating and re-proving step one more time.

8. Deflate the dough and form it into a ball. Leave to rest on the work surface for 5 minutes. Divide into two equal pieces and form into long lengths of about 12" (30cm). Lightly dust a baking tray or 2 baguette pans with flour and carefully transfer the lengths of dough. Cover loosely with floured cheesecloth (muslin). Leave it to rise until it has doubled in size.

9. Meanwhile, place a roasting pan of water in the bottom of the oven, and preheat the oven to 475°F (240°C/220°C fan oven). Using a lame or sharp knife, slash the tops with diagonal slits about ¼" (6mm) deep down the length of the dough, and brush the tops with cold water. Bake in the center of the oven for about 25 minutes, until they are golden, crusty, and sound hollow when tapped underneath. Transfer to a wire rack to cool. Best served warm while the crusts are crisp and the crumb is chewy.

Alternative Method

1. Prove the dough at coolish room temperature instead of the fridge for 2 hours or until it has doubled in size.

2. Deflate, rest, and shape the dough as directed above. Place on a lightly dusted baking tray or in pans. Slash the tops as above and brush with cold water.

3. Carefully place a large roasting pan of very hot water in the bottom of a cold oven and put the loaves on the middle shelf. Close the door, set the oven temperature to 425°F (220°C/200°C fan oven), and bake for about 40 minutes, until they are golden, crusty, and sound hollow when tapped underneath. Cool on a wire rack and serve warm.

White Sourdough

This is a good recipe to get you started on your sourdough adventure. The recipe uses the starter featured in this book and very strong white bread flour, which gives a chewy, lightly aerated crumb with a crisp crust. From this recipe, you should be able to try different blends of flours to achieve your perfect loaf.

Makes: one 2 lb. 2 oz. (950g), 7" (18cm) diameter loaf
Preparation Time: 35 minutes, plus making a starter and proving
Cooking Time: 1 hour

Ingredients

- 1 lb. 2 oz. (500g) very strong white bread flour, plus extra for dusting
- 1½ tsp. salt
- 12 oz. (350g) basic starter (page 49)
- 6–7 fl. oz. (175–200mL) lukewarm water

Directions

1. In a large glass, porcelain, or plastic bowl, mix the flour and salt. Make a well in the center and add the starter (reserve and replenish the remaining starter). Using a wooden spoon, gently mix the starter with a little flour from the edges of the well to form a smooth paste.

2. Gradually pour and mix in sufficient water, carefully stirring in the dry ingredients from the outside of the bowl to form a stiff, sticky, ball-like mixture in the middle of the bowl.

3. Turn the dough onto a lightly floured work surface and knead until smooth and elastic, for about 10 minutes.

4. Put the dough in a large, lightly floured glass, porcelain, or plastic bowl. The bowl needs to be big enough to allow room for the dough to double in size. Cover the bowl with a clean tea towel or cheesecloth (muslin). Ideally, prove overnight in the fridge, then remove the dough from the fridge and stand at room temperature for 2 hours to thoroughly take the chill off. Alternatively, leave it to rise at a coolish room temperature, away from drafts, for about 2 hours or until it has doubled in size.

5. Once the dough has risen satisfactorily, push your knuckles into the dough to deflate it and turn it out onto a lightly floured surface. Form the dough into a ball and let it rest for 5 minutes on the work surface before you shape it.

6. Shape the dough into a neat round about 6" (15cm) and carefully transfer to a large, lightly floured baking tray, seam side down. Cover with a large bowl and set aside to prove in a warm place until it has doubled in size. If using a proving basket, dust the inside with flour and place the shaped dough seam side up in the basket. Cover and prove in the same way.

7. Meanwhile, place a roasting pan of water in the bottom of the oven and preheat the oven to 425°F (220°C/200°C fan oven). Remove the bowl from the dough and using a lame or sharp knife, slash the loaf top about ½" (1cm) deep to your desired design and dust lightly with flour. If basket-proved, carefully flip onto a floured baking tray and slash as above.

8. Bake in the center of the oven for about 1 hour, until golden brown and hollow sounding when tapped underneath. Transfer to a wire rack to cool.

French-Style Sourdough (Couronne)

A starter called *poolish* is used in French bakery products. It ferments for a much shorter period. The resulting bread (*pain de campagne*) has a springy texture with a less-yeasty flavor. Because of the small quantity of yeast required, it is easier to use active dry yeast for this recipe. In this recipe, the dough is shaped and baked as a couronne, or ring-shaped loaf.

Makes: one 2 lb. (900g), 10" (25cm) couronne
Preparation Time: 35 minutes, plus starter making and proving
Cooking Time: 35 minutes

For the Starter

- 7 fl. oz. (200mL) lukewarm water
- ¾ tsp. active dry yeast
- 7 oz. (200g) very strong white bread flour

For the Dough

- 14 oz. (400g) very strong white bread flour
- 3½ oz. (100g) rye flour, plus extra for dusting
- 1½ tsp. salt
- 9 fl. oz. (250mL) lukewarm water

Directions

1. For the poolish, pour the water into a bowl and sprinkle over the yeast. Using a wooden spoon, stir until the yeast dissolves in the water. Add the flour and mix to make a smooth paste. Cover the bowl with another bowl and leave it to ferment at coolish room temperature overnight for up to 2 days. The mixture should be bubbly and smell pleasantly yeasty when ready to use.

2. For the main dough, mix the flours and salt in a large mixing bowl and make a well in the center. Add the poolish and gently mix into the flour using a wooden spoon.

3. Gradually pour and mix in the water, carefully stirring in the dry ingredients from the outside of the bowl to form a stiff, sticky, ball-like mixture in the middle of the bowl.

4. Turn the dough onto a lightly floured work surface and knead until smooth and elastic, for about 10 minutes.

5. Put the dough in a large, lightly floured glass, porcelain, or plastic bowl. The bowl needs to be big enough to allow room for the dough to double in size. Cover the bowl with a clean tea towel or cheesecloth (muslin). Leave it to rise at a coolish room temperature, away from drafts, for about 2 hours or until it has doubled in size.

6. Once the dough has risen satisfactorily, push your knuckles into the dough to deflate it and turn it out onto a lightly floured surface. Form the dough into a ball and let it rest for 5 minutes on the work surface before you shape it.

7. To make a ring-shaped loaf, shape the dough into a round. Using the knuckles of your hand, push down firmly into the center of the dough, right through to the work surface, to make a hole.

8. Lightly push out the dough using stretched fingers to make a hole about 6" (15cm) in diameter. Transfer to a large, lightly floured baking tray, cover with a large bowl and set aside to prove in a warm place until doubled in size.

9. Meanwhile, preheat the oven to 425°F (220°C/200°C fan oven). Remove the cover; if the hole in the center has closed, reform the middle by gently repeating the stretching process. Dust with a little rye flour and bake in the center of the oven for about 35 minutes, until golden, risen, and hollow sounding when tapped underneath. Transfer to a wire rack to cool completely.

French-Style Sourdough Loaf

If preferred, bake the dough as a simple free-form round loaf without forming it into a ring shape.

Ciabatta

The starter used in some Italian breadmaking is called *biga*. It is left to ferment for at least 12 hours. As well as using a starter, you need to add a little extra yeast to the dough to make this popular aerated bread. The yeast quantities are small, so it is easier to use active dry yeast. Ciabatta dough is very soft and sticky, and as such, is not kneaded. Handle it gently and carefully to retain as many of the air bubbles as possible

Makes: two 13 oz. (375g), approx. 11" (28cm) long loaves
Preparation Time: 40 minutes, plus starter making and proving
Cooking Time: 30 minutes

For the Starter

- ½ tsp. active dry yeast
- 5 fl. oz. (150mL) lukewarm water
- ¼ tsp. superfine sugar
- 5 oz. (150g) white bread flour

For the Dough

- 8 fl. oz. (225mL) lukewarm water
- ½ tsp. active dry yeast
- 12 oz. (350g) white bread flour, plus extra for dusting
- 1 tsp. salt
- 1 Tbsp. good-quality olive oil

Directions

1. For the biga, pour the water into a bowl and sprinkle over the yeast. Using a wooden spoon, stir until the yeast dissolves in the water. Add the sugar and flour and mix to make a smooth paste. Cover the bowl with another bowl and leave it to rise and ferment at room temperature for at least 12 hours or overnight. The mixture should be bubbly and smell pleasantly yeasty when ready to use.

2. For the main dough, pour half the water in a small bowl and sprinkle over the yeast. Using a wooden spoon, stir until the yeast dissolves in the water.

3. Mix the flour and salt in a large mixing bowl. Make a well in the center and add the yeasty liquid, biga, and olive oil, and gently mix into the flour using a wooden spoon.

4. Gradually pour and mix in the water, carefully stirring in the dry ingredients from the outside of the bowl to form a soft, sticky mixture in the middle of the bowl.

5. This dough will be too soft to knead, so without adding any flour, use a wooden spoon to gently twist, turn, fold, and stretch the dough in the bowl, for about 5 minutes, until the mixture begins to pull away from the sides of the bowl.

6. Cover the bowl with a clean tea towel or cheesecloth (muslin). Leave to rise at a coolish room temperature, away from drafts, for about 3 hours or until 3 times the size. Do not push or mix the dough at all.

7. Dust 2 large baking trays generously with flour. Using a sharp knife or scraper, cut the dough in half. Flour your hands well, and scoop out half of the dough onto one of the baking trays—use a scraper if preferred. Gently shape into an oblong about 10" (25cm) long, tuck the edges under, and neaten the sides with your fingers. Lightly dust the top with flour.

8. Repeat with the other half of the dough, and leave uncovered to prove in a warm place for 20 minutes to spread and rise.

9. Preheat the oven to 425°F (220°C/200°C fan oven). Bake the loaves for about 30 minutes, swapping them round in the oven halfway through, until risen, golden, and hollow sounding when tapped underneath. Transfer to a wire rack to cool.

Rye Sourdough

There are many varieties of rye bread. Rye is a crop grown in Germany, and this bread is based on a typical German recipe. Use the sourdough starter in this book to make a dense, slightly sour tasting loaf. Leave out the caraway seeds if preferred.

Makes: one 2 lb. (900g), 9" (23cm) long loaf
Preparation Time: 35 minutes, plus making a starter and proving
Cooking Time: 1 hour

Ingredients

- 12 oz. (350g) rye flour, plus extra for dusting
- 5 oz. (150g) very strong bread flour
- 1½ tsp. salt
- 2 tsp. caraway seeds
- 12 oz. (350g) basic starter (page 49)
- 6 fl. oz. (175mL) lukewarm water

Rye on its own makes a heavy bread, so it is best mixed with another flour.

Directions

1. Mix the flours, salt, and seeds in a large mixing bowl. Make a well in the center and add the starter (reserve and replenish the remaining starter) and gently mix using a wooden spoon with a little of the flour to form a smooth paste.

2. Gradually pour and mix in the water, carefully stirring in the dry ingredients from the outside of the bowl to form a stiff, sticky, ball-like mixture in the middle of the bowl.

3. Turn the dough onto a lightly floured work surface and knead until smooth and elastic, for about 10 minutes.

4. Put the dough in a large, lightly floured glass, porcelain, or plastic bowl. The bowl needs to be big enough to allow room for the dough to double in size. Cover the bowl with a clean tea towel or cheesecloth (muslin). Leave it to rise at a coolish room temperature, away from drafts, for about 2 hours or until doubled in size.

5. Once the dough has risen satisfactorily, push your knuckles into the dough to deflate it and turn it out onto a lightly floured surface. Form the dough into a ball and let it rest for 5 minutes on the work surface before you shape it into an 8" (20cm) long loaf. Alternatively, shape to fit a proving basket.

6. Carefully transfer to a large, lightly floured baking tray, seam side down. Cover with a large bowl and set aside to prove in a warm place until it has doubled in size. If using a proving basket, dust the inside with flour and place the shaped dough seam side up in the basket. Cover and prove in the same way.

7. Meanwhile, preheat the oven to 400°F (200°C/180°C fan oven). Remove the bowl and using a lame or sharp knife, slash the loaf about ½" (1cm) deep down its length and dust lightly with rye flour. If basket-proved, carefully flip out on to a floured baking tray.

8. Bake in the center of the oven for about 1 hour, until golden brown and hollow sounding when tapped underneath. Transfer to a wire rack to cool.

Gluten-Free Sourdough

Follow the instructions for making a starter, but use rice flour. The rest of the recipe uses a ready-blended gluten-free all-purpose (plain) flour combined with buckwheat flour for extra flavor. From this basic recipe, you will be able to experiment using your own combination of favorite flours.

Makes: two 1 lb. (500g) loaves

Preparation Time: 20 minutes, plus making a starter, resting, and proving

Cooking Time: 50 minutes

Ingredients

- 7 oz. (200g) gluten-free all-purpose flour
- 7 oz. (200g) buckwheat flour, plus extra to dust
- 1 tsp. salt
- 1 Tbsp. superfine sugar
- 1½ tsp. xanthan gum
- 1 oz. (25g) psyllium husk powder
- 10 oz. (300g) basic gluten-free starter (page 49)
- 2 medium eggs, beaten, or vegan egg (page 34)
- 10 fl. oz (300mL) lukewarm water

Directions

1. Grease and line two 1 lb. (450g) loaf pans. Mix the flours, salt, sugar, xanthan gum, and psyllium husk powder. Make a well in the center and add the starter (reserve and replenish the remaining starter) and eggs or vegan egg. Gently mix using a wooden spoon to form a smooth, thick batter.

2. Gradually pour and mix in the water, carefully stirring in the dry ingredients from the outside of the bowl to form a soft sticky mixture. Rest for 10 minutes, then stir again.

3. Divide the dough equally and transfer to the prepared pans. Smooth the tops, cover with a large bowl, and leave to rise in at a coolish room temperature, away from drafts, for about 2 hours until risen to the top of the pans.

4. Meanwhile, preheat the oven to 400°F (200°C/180°C fan oven). Remove the bowl and using a lame or sharp knife, slash each loaf about ½" (1cm) deep down its length. Dust lightly with flour and bake in the center of the oven for about 50 minutes, until risen, crusty, and golden. The loaves should sound hollow when tapped underneath. Turn out on to a wire rack to cool.

Note
Best eaten with three days of baking or frozen on the same day as baking.

Gluten-Free Oaty Loaf

This is a simple recipe to make a loaf with good flavor and extra texture. From this basic recipe, you will be able to experiment with your own flour blends. The recipe uses instant dry yeast for extra convenience.

Makes: one 1 lb. 14 oz. (850g), 7" (18cm) round loaf
Preparation Time: 20 minutes, plus resting and proving
Cooking Time: 1 hour 10 minutes

Ingredients

- 7 oz. (200g) gluten-free all-purpose flour
- 7 oz. (200g) gluten-free oat flour
- ¼ oz. (7g) sachet instant dry yeast
- 1½ tsp. xanthan gum
- 1 oz. (25g) psyllium husk powder
- 2 tsp. superfine sugar
- 1 tsp. salt
- 2 medium eggs, beaten, or vegan egg (page 34)
- 15 fl. oz. (425mL) lukewarm water
- 1 Tbsp. gluten-free coarse-milled (jumbo) oats

Directions

1. Grease and line a 7" (18cm) diameter, 3" (7.5cm) deep, round cake pan or dish. Mix the flours in a large mixing bowl and stir in the yeast until well combined. Stir in the xanthan gum, psyllium husk powder, sugar, and salt. Make a well in the center.

2. Add the eggs or vegan egg and half the water and mix with a wooden spoon until well blended. Continue adding sufficient water until the mixture is soft and sticky. Leave to rest for 10 minutes, then mix again.

3. Transfer to the prepared pan. Smooth the top, cover with a large bowl, and leave it to rise in at a coolish room temperature, away from drafts, for about 2 hours until risen to the top of the pan.

4. Meanwhile, preheat the oven to 400°F (200°C/180°C fan oven). Remove the bowl, sprinkle over the oats, and bake in the center of the oven for about 1 hour 10 minutes, until risen, crusty, and golden. The loaf should sound hollow when tapped underneath. Turn out on to a wire rack to cool.

Note

Best eaten within three days of baking or frozen on the same day as baking.

Focaccia

A flattish bread that means "hearth" in Italian and originated in Genoa. It can be made with many different additions. This is a basic rosemary-flavored recipe to which you can add your own flavorings.

Makes: one 1 lb. 10 oz. (750g),
9" x 11" (23 x 28cm) rectangular bread

Preparation Time: 40 minutes, plus proving

Cooking Time: 25 minutes

Ingredients

- ½ oz. (15g) fresh yeast or 2 tsp. active dry yeast or ¼ oz. (7g) sachet instant dry yeast
- 9½ fl. oz. (275mL) lukewarm water
- 1 lb. 2 oz. (500g) white bread flour
- 1 Tbsp. freshly chopped rosemary leaves
- 1½ tsp. salt
- 4 Tbsp. (60mL) good-quality olive oil
- 1 tsp. coarse sea salt
- Fresh rosemary, to garnish

Directions

1. Crumble the fresh yeast into a small glass bowl and add 3½ fl. oz. (100mL) of the lukewarm water. Using a wooden spoon, mix the yeast until it dissolves into the water. If using active dry yeast, sprinkle the yeast over the same amount of lukewarm water and proceed as for fresh yeast. If using instant dry yeast, simply mix straight into the flour before adding any water.

2. Mix the flour, rosemary, and salt in a large mixing bowl and make a well in the center. Pour the yeasty liquid in the center of the well, add 2 Tbsp. (30mL) oil and gently mix into the flour using a wooden spoon.

3. Gradually pour and mix in the remaining water, carefully stirring in the dry ingredients from the outside of the bowl to form a softish, ball-like mixture in the middle of the bowl.

4. Turn the dough onto a lightly floured work surface and knead until smooth and elastic, for about 10 minutes.

5. Put the dough in a large lightly oiled glass, porcelain, or plastic bowl. The bowl needs to be big enough to allow room for the dough to double in size. Cover the bowl with a clean tea towel or cheesecloth (muslin). Leave to rise at a coolish room temperature, away from drafts, for about 2 hours or until it has doubled in size.

6. Once the dough has risen satisfactorily, push your knuckles into the dough to deflate it and turn it out onto an unfloured surface. Form the dough into a ball and let it rest for 5 minutes on the work surface before you shape it.

7. Grease a 9" x 11" (23 x 28cm) Swiss roll pan. Roll and stretch the dough until it is big enough to fit the pan. Continue to press the dough once it is in the pan until it reaches the corners. Cover with a clean tea towel or cheesecloth (muslin). Leave to prove in a warm place until doubled in size.

8. Meanwhile, preheat the oven to 425°F (220°C/200°C fan oven). Remove the covering and use your fingertips to make indents all over the dough. Brush with remaining oil, sprinkle with salt, and bake in the center of the oven for about 25 minutes, until golden brown and hollow sounding when tapped underneath. Cool for 10 minutes before turning out on to a wire rack to cool. Best served warm, sprinkled with fresh rosemary.

Gluten-Free Focaccia

1. Mix 10 oz. (300g) gluten-free white bread flour with ¾ oz. (20g) gram (garbanzo bean or chickpea) flour, ½ tsp. salt, 2 tsp. chopped rosemary, and ¼ oz. (7g) sachet instant dry yeast.

2. Make a well in the center and add 4 Tbsp. (60mL) olive oil and 7 fl. oz. (200mL) lukewarm water. Mix to make a soft, sticky dough.

3. Cover as above and rest for 15 minutes. Press into a lightly greased 8" (20cm) square cake pan, cover with a bowl, and leave to rise at room temperature for about 2 hours until risen.

4. Make indents as above, brush with a little more olive oil, sprinkle with a little coarse salt, and bake as above for about 40 minutes. Cool for 20 minutes before removing from the pan. Best served warm.

Steamed Sesame Buns

Steamed wheat buns have their origins in northern China. The bread is soft and silky with no crust because it is cooked without direct heat. Today, steamed buns are a popular street food and are filled with a vast range of fillings and sauces. This simplified version uses instant dry yeast and is flavored with sesame oil.

Makes: four 3½ oz. (100g) buns
Preparation Time: 30 minutes, plus proving
Cooking Time: 35 minutes

Ingredients

- 9 oz. (250g) all-purpose flour, plus extra for dusting
- 1 tsp. instant dry yeast
- ¼ tsp. salt
- ¼ tsp. baking powder
- 1 tsp. superfine sugar
- 1 Tbsp. sesame oil
- 4½ fl. oz. (125mL) lukewarm 2% dairy or plant-based milk, plus extra for glazing
- 2 tsp. white-and-black sesame seeds

Directions

1. Mix the flour, yeast, salt, baking powder, and sugar together in a mixing bowl and make a well in the center. Add 2 tsp. sesame oil and pour in the milk, and gently mix using a wooden spoon to make a soft dough.

2. Turn out on to a lightly floured work surface. Knead for about 5 minutes, until soft and smooth.

3. Put the dough in a large, lightly floured glass, porcelain, or plastic bowl. The bowl needs to be big enough to allow room for the dough to double in size. Cover the bowl with a clean tea towel or cheesecloth (muslin). Leave to rise at a coolish room temperature, away from drafts, for about 2 hours or until it has doubled in size.

4. Once the dough has risen satisfactorily, push your knuckles into the dough to deflate it and turn it out onto an unfloured surface. Knead for 1 minute. Form the dough into a ball and let it rest for 5 minutes on the work surface.

5. Divide the dough into 4 equal pieces and shape each into a small ball. Working on 1 piece of dough at a time, roll into an oval shape about 6" x 3½" (15 x 9cm). Peel away from the surface and place on a lightly floured board. Brush lightly with a little of the remaining sesame oil and fold loosely in half—do not press down.

6. When you have shaped all the pieces, cover as before, and leave in a warm place for about 35 minutes, until slightly risen and puffed. Brush with a little milk and sprinkle with seeds.

7. Put a steamer over a large pan of boiling water. Arrange the buns spaced a little apart on baking paper in the steamer, cover with the lid, and steam for about 30 minutes, until risen and cooked through. Keep warm to serve immediately or cool on a wire rack for later use.

To Reheat

Steam the buns as above for about 5 minutes, until warm or pop them in the microwave for a few seconds.

Gluten-Free Steamed Buns

It is easier to make round buns with a gluten-free dough. Use a ready-prepared blend of gluten-free all-purpose flour if preferred, but the combination below gives a pleasantly chewy texture.

1. Mix 2½ oz. (70g) each of cornstarch, tapioca flour, white rice flour and glutinous rice flour in a large mixing bowl. Stir in salt, gluten-free baking powder, superfine sugar, and instant dry yeast as above.

2. Add 2 tsp. sesame oil and approx. 13 Tbsp. (190mL) lukewarm dairy or plant milk, and mix to make a softish but manageable dough. Cover and stand for 10 minutes. Divide into four and shape into 3½" (9cm) flattish rounds. Place on an oiled baking tray. Cover as above and leave for about 1 hour until risen.

3. Brush with milk and sprinkle with seeds as above. Steam as above for about 35 minutes, until risen and firm to the touch. The outside will be a little sticky. Cool for about 45 minutes before slicing with a serrated knife. Best served warm.

Bagels

The famous Jewish bread roll, popular with everyone. Best made and eaten as fresh as possible, but they do freeze well—cool, wrap tightly, and freeze for up to three months.

Makes: eight 3½ oz. (100g) bagels

Preparation Time: 50 minutes, plus proving

Cooking Time: 27 minutes

Ingredients

- ½ oz. (15g) fresh yeast or 2 tsp. active dry yeast or ¼ oz. (7g) sachet instant dry yeast
- 9½ fl. oz. (275mL) lukewarm water
- 1 lb. 3 oz. (550g) white bread flour, plus extra for dusting
- 2 Tbsp. (25g) superfine sugar
- 2 tsp. salt
- 2 Tbsp. (30mL) sunflower oil
- 1 egg yolk mixed with 1 Tbsp. water, or vegan glaze (page 59)
- 2 Tbsp. (18g) poppy seeds, sesame seeds, or dried onion pieces (optional)

Directions

1. Crumble the fresh yeast into a small glass bowl and add 3½ fl. oz. (100mL) of the lukewarm water. Using a wooden spoon, mix the yeast until it dissolves into the water. If using active dry yeast, sprinkle the yeast over the same amount of lukewarm water, and proceed as for fresh yeast. If using instant dry yeast, simply mix straight into the flour before adding any water.

2. Mix all but 1½ oz. (40g) flour, sugar, and salt in a large mixing bowl, and make a well in the center. Pour the yeasty water in the center of the well along with the oil and gently mix using a wooden spoon.

3. Gradually pour and mix in the remaining water, carefully stirring in the dry ingredients from the outside of the bowl to form a firm, moist, ball-like mixture in the middle of the bowl.

4. Generously flour the work surface with the remaining flour and turn the dough onto it. Knead until smooth and elastic, for about 10 minutes, gradually adding all the surface flour to make a very firm dough.

5. Put the dough in a large, lightly floured glass, porcelain, or plastic bowl. The bowl needs to be big enough to allow room for the dough to double in size. Cover the bowl with a clean tea towel or cheesecloth (muslin). Leave it to rise at a coolish room temperature, away from drafts, for about 2 hours until it has doubled in size.

6. Once the dough has risen satisfactorily, push your knuckles into the dough to deflate it and turn it out onto a lightly floured surface. Form the dough into a ball and let it rest for 5 minutes on the work surface.

7. Divide the dough into 8 equal pieces and shape each into a smooth round. Lightly grease the end of a wooden spoon and press through the center of each, wiggling the spoon around to stretch and enlarge the hole in the center.

8. Carefully transfer to an oiled baking tray, spaced well apart, and cover with oiled greaseproof paper and then cheesecloth (muslin). Leave in a warm place to prove for about 20 minutes, until just starting to rise. Take care not to let the rings rise too much, otherwise they will become misshapen. Open the center hole again if necessary, using the wooden spoon handle.

9. Meanwhile, preheat the oven to 425°F (220°C/200°C fan oven). Bring a large deep sided frying pan of water to the boil and reduce to a gentle simmer. Poach 4 bagels at a time, in the water for 1 minute on 1 side only. Remove with a slotted spoon and place on a large lightly greased baking tray. Repeat with the remaining bagels.

10. Brush all over with an egg yolk or vegan glaze, and sprinkle lightly with seeds if using. Bake in the center of the oven for about 25 minutes, until richly golden. Transfer to a wire rack to cool. Best served warm.

Pitas

These much-loved snack breads are straightforward to make. Known as pitas in Greece and *khubz* in the Middle East, they keep for a few days and can be simply reheated by popping in the toaster for a few seconds to warm through before eating.

Makes: eight 3¼ oz. (90g), 7" (18cm) long breads
Preparation Time: 45 minutes, plus proving
Cooking Time: 15 minutes

Ingredients

- ½ oz. (15g) fresh yeast or 2 tsp. active dry yeast or ¼ oz. (7g) sachet instant dry yeast
- 9½ fl. oz. (275mL) lukewarm water
- 1 lb. 2 oz. (500g) white bread flour
- 1 tsp. salt
- 1 tsp. superfine sugar
- 2 Tbsp. (30mL) good-quality olive oil

Directions

1. Crumble the fresh yeast into a small glass bowl and add 3½ fl. oz. (100mL) of the lukewarm water. Using a wooden spoon, mix the yeast until it dissolves into the water. If using active dry yeast, sprinkle the yeast over the same amount of lukewarm water and proceed as for fresh yeast. If using instant dry yeast, simply mix straight into the flour before adding any water.

2. Mix flour, salt, and sugar in a large mixing bowl and make a well in the center. Pour the yeasty water into the center of the well. Add the oil and gently mix using a wooden spoon.

3. Gradually pour and mix in the remaining water, carefully stirring in the dry ingredients from the outside of the bowl to form a firmish, moist mixture in the middle of the bowl.

4. Turn the dough onto a lightly floured work surface and knead until smooth and elastic, for about 10 minutes.

5. Put the dough in a large lightly oiled glass, porcelain, or plastic bowl. The bowl needs to be big enough to allow room for the dough to double in size. Cover the bowl with a clean tea towel or cheesecloth (muslin). Leave it to rise at a coolish room temperature, away from drafts, for about 2 hours or it has until doubled in size.

6. Once the dough has risen satisfactorily, push your knuckles into the dough to deflate it and turn it out onto an unfloured surface. Form the dough into a ball and let it rest for 5 minutes on the work surface.

7. Divide the dough into eight equal pieces and shape each piece into a smooth ball. Roll each piece into a thin oval shape about 9" (23cm) long. Peel away from the work surface and place on a floured board. Cover as above and leave in a warm place to prove for about 20 minutes, until just risen and slightly puffy.

8. Meanwhile, preheat the oven to 425°F (220°C/200°C fan oven). Dust 2 baking trays lightly with flour and heat for 5 minutes. Remove the covering from the breads, carefully transfer the breads to the trays, and bake for about 15 minutes, swapping the trays halfway through, until puffy and very lightly browned. Wrap the hot breads in clean, dry cheesecloth (muslin) to keep the crusts soft and prevent them from drying out. Best served warm.

Variation

For whole wheat breads, replace half the flour with whole wheat bread flour.

Grissini

An essential for antipasto or for eating as a delicious crisp and crunchy snack, breadsticks are popular with every age group. It is easier to use active dry yeast for this recipe.

Makes: forty 10" (25cm) long breadsticks
Preparation Time: 50 minutes, plus resting
Cooking Time: 10 minutes

Ingredients

- 5 fl. oz. (150mL) lukewarm water
- 1 tsp. active dry yeast or 1 tsp. instant dry yeast
- ½ tsp. superfine sugar
- 9 oz. (250g) white bread flour, plus extra for dusting
- 1 tsp. salt
- 1 Tbsp. good-quality olive oil

Directions

1. Pour half the water into a bowl and sprinkle over the active dry yeast. Stir in the sugar. If using instant dry yeast, simply mix into the flour with the sugar and salt before adding any water.

2. Mix the flour and salt in a mixing bowl and make a well in the center. Add the yeasty liquid and the olive oil to the center of the well and gently mix into the flour using a wooden spoon.

3. Gradually pour and mix in the remaining water, carefully stirring in the dry ingredients from the outside of the bowl to form a softish, ball-like mixture in the middle of the bowl.

4. Turn the dough onto an unfloured work surface and knead until smooth and elastic, for about 10 minutes. Rest for 10 minutes, then knead again for a further 10 minutes.

5. Roll and shape the dough into an 8" x 10" (20 x 25cm) rectangle. Cover with cheesecloth (muslin) and rest for 10 minutes.

6. Meanwhile, preheat the oven to 425°F (220°C/200°C fan oven). Lightly sprinkle 2 or 3 large baking trays with flour. Cut the dough lengthways into (20) 10" (25cm) long strips. As you pull each strip away from the work top, gently stretch it to double its length, and cut in half. Arrange on the baking trays spaced a little apart. Dust lightly with flour if preferred and bake for 10 minutes, swapping the trays halfway through, until golden and crisp. Transfer to a wire rack to cool.

Grissini Variations

For thicker breadsticks, bake the strips without stretching beyond 10" (25cm). They will need 15–20 minutes in the oven to crisp. Add flavor by brushing with the flavored oil before baking or brush with the egg or vegan glaze and sprinkle with seeds, herbs, or salt.

Naan

Traditionally these delicious flat breads are cooked in a clay tandoor oven that gives them a quick blast of high heat and light charring. This recipe shows you how to achieve similar results using a traditional oven and grill.

Makes: four 6 oz. (175g), 10" (25cm) long breads
Preparation Time: 40 minutes, plus proving
Cooking Time: 8 minutes

Ingredients

- ½ oz. (15g) fresh yeast or 2 tsp. active dry yeast or ¼ oz. (7g) sachet instant dry yeast
- 6 fl. oz. (175mL) lukewarm water
- 3½ oz. (100g) whole milk plain (natural) or plant-based yogurt
- 1 lb. 2 oz. (500g) white bread flour
- 1½ tsp. salt
- 1 tsp. superfine sugar
- 2 tsp. black onion seeds (optional)
- 3 oz. (75g) unsalted dairy or plant-based butter, melted

Directions

1. Crumble the fresh yeast into a small glass bowl and add 3½ fl. oz. (100mL) of the lukewarm water. Using a wooden spoon, mix the yeast until it dissolves into the water. If using active dry yeast, sprinkle the yeast over the same amount of lukewarm water and proceed as for fresh yeast. If using instant dry yeast, simply mix straight into the flour before adding any water.

2. Mix flour, salt, sugar, and seeds, if using, in a large mixing bowl and make a well in the center. Pour the yeasty water into the center of the well. Add the milk or yogurt and 3 Tbsp. (45mL) melted butter. Gently mix into the flour using a wooden spoon.

3. Gradually pour and mix in the remaining water, carefully stirring in the dry ingredients from the outside of the bowl to form a firmish, moist mixture in the middle of the bowl.

4. Turn the dough onto a lightly floured work surface and knead until smooth and elastic, for about 10 minutes.

5. Put the dough in a large, lightly floured glass, porcelain, or plastic bowl. The bowl needs to be big enough to allow room for the dough to double in size. Cover the bowl with a clean tea towel or cheesecloth (muslin). Leave to rise at a coolish room temperature, away from drafts, for about 2 hours or until it has doubled in size.

6. Once the dough has risen satisfactorily, push your knuckles into the dough to deflate it and turn it out onto an unfloured surface. Form the dough into a ball and let it rest for 5 minutes on the work surface.

7. Preheat the oven to 475°F (240°C/220°C fan oven). Divide the dough into four equal pieces and shape each piece into a smooth ball. Roll each piece into a 6" (15cm) diameter round, then pull and stretch one side to form a tear-shaped loaf about 10" (25cm) long.

8. Heat 2 baking trays for 2 minutes in the oven before carefully laying two breads per tray, side by side. Brush with remaining butter and bake for about 8 minutes until it is puffed and golden around the edges.

9. For a browner finish, transfer the baked naans to a grill rack and flash under a preheated hot grill for a few seconds on each side to brown and blister.

10. Wrap the hot breads in clean, dry cheesecloth (muslin) to keep them soft and prevent them from drying. Best served warm.

Brioche

Traditionally, brioche is a buttery enriched French loaf baked in a specialist, fluted pan. This version is made more simply in a 2 lb. (900g) loaf pan. Brioche mixture can also be baked as a popular bun for burgers and other fillings.

Makes: one 1 lb. 6 oz. (625g) loaf

Preparation Time: 50 minutes, plus proving

Cooking Time: 40 minutes

Ingredients

- 1½ tsp. active dry yeast or 1½ tsp. instant dry yeast
- 3 Tbsp. (45mL) lukewarm dairy or plant milk
- 12 oz. (350g) white bread flour
- ¾ tsp. salt
- 1½ oz. (40g) superfine sugar
- 3 medium eggs, beaten, or vegan egg (page 34)
- 3 oz. (75g) unsalted dairy or plant butter, very soft
- 1 egg yolk mixed with 1 Tbsp. water, or vegan glaze (page 59)

Directions

1. Spoon the lukewarm milk into a small bowl and sprinkle over the active dry yeast, stir with a wooden spoon until dissolved in the milk. If using instant dry yeast, simply mix straight into the flour before adding any milk.

2. Mix the flour, salt, and sugar in a large mixing bowl and make a well in the center. Pour the yeasty milk in the center of the well along with the beaten eggs or vegan egg and gently mix using a wooden spoon, stirring in the dry ingredients from the outside of the bowl to form a soft, sticky, ball-like mixture in the middle of the bowl. If using vegan egg, you may need to add a little extra water if the mixture is very stiff.

3. Turn the dough onto a lightly floured work surface and knead until smooth and elastic, for about 10 minutes.

4. Grease a large glass, porcelain, or plastic bowl and put the dough in the bowl. The bowl needs to be big enough to allow room for the dough to double in size. Cover the bowl with a clean tea towel or cheesecloth (muslin). Leave it to rise at a coolish room temperature, away from drafts, for about 2 hours until it has doubled in size.

5. Once the dough has risen satisfactorily, push your knuckles into the dough to deflate it and turn it out onto a lightly floured surface. Form the dough into a ball and let it rest for 5 minutes on the work surface.

6. Flatten the dough slightly and then spread the top with the butter. Gradually work the butter into the dough by squeezing the dough with your hands. Knead for 5 minutes to make sure the butter is thoroughly blended throughout the dough, then form into a smooth round ball. Rest for 5 minutes.

7. Grease a 2 lb. (900g) loaf pan. Divide the dough into 8 equal portions and form each into a neat ball. Arrange the balls in the pan seam side down, 4 to each side, pressing them gently to make them fit. Cover as above and leave to prove in a warm place until doubled in size.

8. Preheat the oven to 400°F (200°C/180°C fan oven). Remove the covering and brush all over with the glaze. Bake in the center of the oven for 40 minutes, until richly golden, well risen, and hollow sounding when tapped underneath. Cover with foil if the brioche browns too quickly. Turn out on to a wire rack to cool. Best served warm.

Brioche Buns

You can use this dough to make 10 rolls, following the directions for Basic White Bread Rolls (page 80). Glaze, sprinkle with sesame seeds, and bake as in step 8 for 20-25 minutes.

Doughnuts

Today a well-known branded fast-food snack, this old-fashioned-style doughnut is one of the best bready treats around. Crunchy on the outside with a fluffy dough on the inside. Fill with your favorite jam or spread, or a chunk of chocolate if you like, but they are just as enjoyable left plain.

Makes: ten 2 oz. (50g) doughnuts

Preparation Time: 45 minutes, plus proving

Cooking Time: 15 minutes

Ingredients

- ½ oz. (15g) fresh yeast or 2 tsp. active dry yeast or ¼ oz. (7g) sachet instant dry yeast
- 4 fl. oz. (115mL) lukewarm dairy or plant milk
- 10 oz. (300g) white bread flour
- ½ tsp. salt
- 3 oz. (75g) superfine sugar
- 1 oz. (25g) unsalted dairy or plant butter, melted
- 1 medium egg, beaten or vegan egg (page 34)
- 2½ oz. (70g) smooth jam or spread, or 10 small chunks of chocolate (optional)
- Vegetable oil for deep frying

Adding a filling of your favorite jam or jelly will make these doughy delights even more delicious.

Directions

1. Crumble the fresh yeast into a small glass bowl and add the lukewarm milk. Using a wooden spoon, mix the yeast until it dissolves into the milk. If using active dry yeast, sprinkle the yeast over the lukewarm milk and proceed as for fresh yeast. If using instant dry yeast, simply mix straight into the flour before adding any milk.

2. Mix the flour, salt, and 1 oz. (25g) sugar in a large mixing bowl and make a well in the center. Pour in the yeasty milk. Add the butter and egg and gently mix into the flour using a wooden spoon, carefully stirring in the dry ingredients from the outside of the bowl to form a softish, ball-like mixture in the middle of the bowl.

3. Turn the dough onto a lightly floured work surface and knead until smooth and elastic, and the dough no longer sticks to the work surface, for about 10 minutes.

4. Put the dough in a large lightly oiled glass, porcelain, or plastic bowl. The bowl needs to be big enough to allow room for the dough to double in size. Cover the bowl with a clean tea towel or cheesecloth (muslin). Leave it to rise at a coolish room temperature, away from drafts, for about 2 hours until it has doubled in size.

5. Once the dough has risen satisfactorily, push your knuckles into the dough to deflate it and turn it out onto a lightly floured surface. Form the dough into a ball and let it rest for 5 minutes on the work surface.

6. Divide the dough into 10 pieces, and form each into a ball. If filling, on the seam side, push your thumbs into the center to hollow out and make a dome shape. Add ½ tsp. jam or spread, or a small chunk of chocolate. Then gather up the edges and pinch together to enclose the filling completely. Reshape into balls.

7. Arrange spaced apart, on a well-oiled baking or plastic tray. Cover as above and set aside in a warm place to prove for 30–40 minutes, until doubled in size.

8. Meanwhile, heat the oil for deep frying in a large saucepan to 350°F (180°C). Deep fry three to four doughnuts at a time in the oil for 4–5 minutes, turning them in the oil, until puffed up and richly golden brown. Drain well and then dredge in the remaining caster sugar while warm. Best eaten on the same day as making.

Chocolate Bread

A rich, dark bread, delicious cut in thin slices, and spread with mascarpone, ricotta cheese, or chocolate spread. If you like nuts, replace the chocolate chips with chopped, toasted hazelnuts, walnuts or almonds. Or use chopped dried fruit instead.

Makes: one 1 lb. 14 oz. (850g), 7" (18cm) round loaf

Preparation Time: 35 minutes

Cooking Time: 45 minutes

Ingredients

- ½ oz. (15g) fresh yeast or 2 tsp. active dry yeast or ¼ oz. (7g) sachet instant dry yeast
- 9½ fl. oz. (275mL) lukewarm whole milk
- 15 oz. (425g) white bread flour
- ½ tsp. salt
- 1 oz. (25g) cocoa powder
- 1 oz. (25g) dark brown sugar, free of lumps
- 1 oz. (25g) unsalted dairy or plant butter, melted
- 3½ oz. (100g) plain chocolate chips
- 1 egg white, beaten or 2 Tbsp. (30mL) plant-based milk
- 1 Tbsp. superfine sugar

Directions

1. Crumble the fresh yeast into a small glass bowl and add 3½ fl. oz. (100mL) of the lukewarm milk. Using a wooden spoon, mix the yeast until it dissolves into the milk. If using active dry yeast, sprinkle the yeast over the same amount of lukewarm milk and proceed as for fresh yeast. If using instant dry yeast, simply mix straight into the flour before adding any milk.

2. Put the flour and salt in a bowl and sift the cocoa on top. Stir in the brown sugar and make a well in the center. Pour the yeasty milk in the center of the well and add the melted butter. Gently mix using a wooden spoon to form a smooth paste.

3. Gradually pour and mix in the remaining milk, carefully stirring in the dry ingredients from the outside of the bowl to form a softish, ball-like mixture in the center of the bowl.

4. Turn on to a lightly floured surface and knead until smooth and elastic, for about 10 minutes.

5. Toward the end of the kneading time, flatten the dough slightly, and pile the chocolate chips on top. Fold over the dough and continue kneading until well blended.

6. Put the dough in a large, lightly oiled glass, porcelain, or plastic bowl. The bowl needs to be big enough to allow room for the dough to double in size. Cover the bowl with a clean tea towel or cheesecloth (muslin). Leave it to rise at a coolish room temperature, away from drafts, for about 2 hours until it has doubled in size.

7. Once the dough has risen satisfactorily, push your knuckles into the dough to deflate it and turn it out onto a lightly floured surface. Form the dough into a ball and let it rest for 5 minutes on the work surface.

8. Shape the dough into a round loaf. Transfer to a lightly greased baking tray, cover with a bowl and set aside in a warm place to prove for about 1 hour until doubled in size.

9. Meanwhile, preheat the oven to 400°F (200°C/180°C fan oven). Remove the bowl using a lame or sharp knife, cut a slash in the loaf top about ½" (1cm) deep in your chosen design. Brush the loaf with egg white or milk and sprinkle with superfine sugar. Bake in the center of the oven for about 45 minutes, until well risen, crusted with sugar, and hollow sounding when tapped underneath. Transfer to a wire rack to cool. Delicious served warm or cold.

Variation

The loaf is not overly sweet, which makes it an unusual accompaniment to a chili, beef, or rich game stew. Leave out the chocolate chips and the sugar glaze if you plan to serve it with a savory meal.

Christmas Bread

In many countries around the world, special breads are made at Christmas time: panettone in Italy, *julekake* in Norway, and stollen in Germany. This recipe brings together some of the traditional ingredients used to flavor festive breads to create a simple loaf that looks very impressive with its fruity, swirled dough.

Makes: one 2 lb. 3½ oz. (1kg) loaf
Preparation Time: 40 minutes, plus proving
Cooking Time: 55 minutes

Ingredients

- ½ oz. (15g) fresh yeast or 2 tsp. active dry yeast or ¼ oz. (7g) sachet instant dry yeast
- 9½ fl. oz. (275mL) lukewarm dairy or plant milk
- 1 lb. 2 oz. (500g) white bread flour
- ¾ tsp. salt
- ½ tsp. ground cardamom
- Finely grated rind of 1 orange

- 2 oz. (50g) unsalted plant or dairy butter, very soft
- 5 oz. (150g) marzipan, grated
- 6 oz. (175g) assorted dried fruits, glacé cherries and chopped nuts
- 1 egg, beaten, or 2 Tbsp. (30mL) vegan glaze (page 59)

Dried fruits, such as raisins, currants, and sultanas, will add a burst of flavor to this bread.

Directions

1. Crumble the fresh yeast into a small glass bowl and add 3½ fl. oz. (100mL) of the lukewarm milk. Using a wooden spoon, mix the yeast until it dissolves into the milk. If using active dry yeast, sprinkle the yeast over the same amount of lukewarm milk and proceed as for fresh yeast. If using instant dry yeast, simply mix straight into the flour before adding any milk.

2. Mix the flour, salt, cardamom, and orange rind in a large mixing bowl and make a well in the center. Pour in the yeasty milk and gently mix into the flour using a wooden spoon.

3. Gradually pour and mix in the remaining milk, carefully stirring in the dry ingredients from the outside of the bowl to form a softish, ball-like mixture in the center of the bowl.

4. Turn on to a lightly floured surface and knead until smooth and elastic, for about 10 minutes.

5. Put the dough in a large lightly floured glass, porcelain, or plastic bowl. The bowl needs to be big enough to allow room for the dough to double in size. Cover the bowl with a clean tea towel or cheesecloth (muslin). Leave it to rise at a coolish room temperature, away from drafts, for about 2 hours until it has doubled in size.

6. Once the dough has risen satisfactorily, push your knuckles into the dough to deflate it and turn it out onto an unfloured surface. Form the dough into a ball and let it rest for five minutes on the work surface. Grease a 2lb (900g) loaf pan.

7. Roll out and stretch the dough smooth side down to make a rectangle 10" x 16" (25 x 40cm), and spread the butter all over the dough right to the edges. Sprinkle the marzipan and the fruit and nuts evenly on top.

8. Carefully peel the dough from the work surface, roll up from the shorter side like a jelly (Swiss) roll, and press gently to seal the underside edge. Tuck the open ends underneath so that the dough will fit the pan, then place seam side down in the prepared pan. Cover as above and set aside in a warm place to prove for about 1 hour until doubled in size.

9. Meanwhile, preheat the oven to 400°F (200°C/180°C fan oven). Remove the covering and brush the loaf with glaze. Bake in the center of the oven for about 55 minutes, until well risen, golden, and hollow sounding when tapped underneath.

10. As soon as the bread is cooked, transfer to a wire rack and leave to cool.

Carrot and Cumin Loaf

A golden loaf with a tempting, savory flavor. It is perfect accompanied with humus or nut spreads. This basic reference recipe will enable you to use all sorts of vegetables in your bread doughs. See the list of suggestions at the end of the recipe.

Makes: one 1 lb. 12 oz. (800g), approx. 5" x 9" (13 x 23cm) oval loaf
Preparation Time: 35 minutes
Cooking Time: 50 minutes

Ingredients

- ½ oz. (15g) fresh yeast or 2 tsp. active dry yeast or ¼ oz. (7g) sachet instant dry yeast
- 2 fl. oz. (50mL) lukewarm water
- 1 lb. 2 oz. (500g) Granary malted brown bread flour or country grain, malted wheat grain, or malthouse flour, plus extra for dusting
- 1½ tsp. salt
- 2 tsp. cumin seeds, toasted and crushed
- 1 Tbsp. sunflower oil
- 3½ oz. (100g) grated carrot
- 6 fl. oz. (175mL) carrot juice, at room temperature

Directions

1. Crumble the fresh yeast into a small glass bowl and add the lukewarm water. Using a wooden spoon, mix the yeast until it dissolves into the water. If using active dry yeast, sprinkle the yeast over the lukewarm water and proceed as for fresh yeast. If using instant dry yeast, simply mix straight into the flour before adding any water.

2. Mix the flour, salt, and half the cumin in a large mixing bowl and make a well in the center. Pour in the yeasty water and gently mix into the flour using a wooden spoon.

3. Add the oil and carrot, and gradually pour and mix in the carrot juice, carefully stirring in the dry ingredients from the outside of the bowl to form a softish, ball-like mixture in the center of the bowl.

4. Turn on to a lightly floured surface and knead until smooth and elastic, for about 10 minutes.

5. Put the dough in a large lightly oiled glass, porcelain, or plastic bowl. The bowl needs to be big enough to allow room for the dough to double in size. Cover the bowl with a clean tea towel or cheesecloth (muslin). Leave it to rise at a coolish room temperature, away from drafts, for about 2 hours until it has doubled in size.

6. Once the dough has risen satisfactorily, push your knuckles into the dough to deflate it and turn it out onto a lightly floured surface. Form the dough into a ball and let it rest for 5 minutes on the work surface before you shape it.

7. Generously flour an oval proving basket with a 8" (20cm) long base. Shape the dough into an 8" (20cm) oval and place it, seam side up, in the basket. Cover with a large bowl and leave to prove in a warm place until doubled in size. Alternatively, shape the dough into an oval, and place seam side down on a floured baking tray. Cover and prove as above.

8. Meanwhile, preheat the oven to 425°F (220°C/200°C fan oven). Remove the bowl covering the loaf, and using a lame or sharp knife, cut a slash the loaf top about ½" (1cm) deep in your chosen design. Bake in the center of the oven for about 50 minutes, until golden brown and hollow sounding when tapped underneath. Turn out on to a wire rack to cool.

Carrot and Cumin Bread Rolls

You can use this dough to make 10 rolls, following the directions for Basic White Bread Rolls (page 80). Glaze and bake as below for 20–25 minutes.

Vegetable Variations

Replace the grated carrot with the same amount of cooked and smoothly mashed potato, sweet potato, beetroot, or parsnip. If you prefer not to use vegetable juice, simply replace with more lukewarm water.

Air Fryer Cheese and Onion Buns

What revolutionary gadgets the air fryer and multicookers are. Adapting conventional recipes to these speedy cookers can sometimes be a challenge, so this recipe should help give you an idea of how to proceed. These buns are perfect for kids to snack on or as an accompaniment to vegetable soup. Delicious warm or cold, plain, or toasted.

Makes: eight 2 oz. (50g) buns

Preparation Time: 35 minutes, plus proving

Cooking Time: 23 minutes

Ingredients

- 9 oz. (250g) soft-grain bread flour or Granary malted brown bread flour, country grain, malted wheat grain, or malthouse flour
- 1 tsp. instant dry yeast
- ½ tsp. salt
- 2 oz. (50g) grated Parmesan cheese
- 5 fl. oz. (150mL) lukewarm water
- 2 scallions, trimmed and finely chopped
- 1 oz. (25g) Monterey Jack or sharp cheddar cheese, grated

Directions

1. Mix the flour, yeast, salt, and Parmesan cheese together in a mixing bowl and make a well in the center. Gradually pour and mix in the water using a wooden spoon, carefully stirring in the dry ingredients from the outside of the bowl to form a softish, ball-like mixture in the center of the bowl.

2. Turn on to a lightly floured surface and knead until smooth and elastic, for about 10 minutes.

3. Toward the end of the kneading time, flatten the dough slightly and pile the chopped scallions on top, then fold over the dough and continue kneading until well blended.

4. Put the dough in a large, lightly oiled glass, porcelain, or plastic bowl. The bowl needs to be big enough to allow room for the dough to double in size. Cover the bowl with a clean tea towel or cheesecloth (muslin). Leave it to rise at a coolish room temperature, away from drafts, for about 2 hours until it has doubled in size.

5. Once the dough has risen satisfactorily, push your knuckles into the dough to deflate it and turn it out onto a lightly floured surface. Form the dough into a ball and let it rest for 5 minutes on the work surface before you shape it.

6. Divide the dough into 8 equal pieces and shape each into a small ball.

7. Remove the air fryer basket from the machine and line with baking parchment or an air fryer liner. Place one ball in the center of the basket and arrange the other balls, just touching around it, as far away from the sides of the basket as possible. Cover as above and leave to prove in a warm place for about 40 minutes, until doubled in size.

8. Remove the covering, place the basket back in the machine and close. Set the temperature to 350°F (180°C) and bake for about 20 minutes, until risen and richly golden brown. Sprinkle over the grated cheese and bake for a further 2–3 minutes, until melted and the buns are hollow sounding when tapped underneath. Transfer to a wire rack to cool and serve warm or cold.

> **Note**
> This recipe was tested in an air fryer basket with an internal dimension of 7½" x 8¾" (19 x 22cm). You may need to adapt the quantity or size of the dough balls to fit your own appliance.

A Very Slow Loaf

Yes, you really can bake bread in a slow cooker! It takes a bit of extra time, but the texture is improved by a long overnight proving, and this makes for a very tasty loaf indeed. Use very strong bread flour for best results. You won't get a natural crust on top of your loaf, but if you prefer, a quick flash under the grill is all you need to achieve one.

Makes: one 1 lb. 11 oz. (775g) round or oval loaf

Preparation Time: 30 minutes,
plus overnight proving and acclimatizing

Cooking Time: 3½ to 4 hours

Ingredients

- ½ oz. (15g) fresh yeast or 2 tsp. active dry yeast or ¼ oz. (7g) sachet instant dry yeast
- 11 fl. oz. (325mL) lukewarm water
- 1 lb. 2 oz. (500g) very strong white bread flour
- 1½ tsp. salt
- 2 oz. (50g) toasted seeds (optional)

Directions

Note

This recipe was tested in an oval slow cooker dish with a 10½ pints (5L) capacity. The temperature when set on high was 250°F (120°C). You may need to adapt the quantity or size of the dough to fit your own appliance and adjust the cooking time if necessary.

1. Crumble the fresh yeast into a small glass bowl and add 3½ fl. oz. (100mL) of the lukewarm water. Using a wooden spoon, mix the yeast until it dissolves into the water. If using active dry yeast, sprinkle the yeast over the same amount of lukewarm water and proceed as for fresh yeast. If using instant dry yeast, simply mix straight into the flour before adding any water.

2. Mix the flour, salt, and seeds if using in a large mixing bowl and make a well in the center. Pour in the yeasty water and gently mix into the flour using a wooden spoon.

3. Gradually pour and mix in the remaining water, carefully stirring in the dry ingredients from the outside of the bowl to form a softish, ball-like mixture in the middle of the bowl.

4. Turn the dough onto a lightly floured work surface and knead until smooth and elastic, for about 10 minutes.

5. Put the dough in a large, lightly oiled glass, porcelain, or plastic bowl. The bowl needs to be big enough to allow room for the dough to double in size. Cover the bowl with another large bowl or domed lid. Leave it overnight in the fridge until it has doubled in size.

6. The next day, remove the dough from the fridge and stand at room temperature for 2 hours to thoroughly take the chill off. Then push your knuckles into the dough to deflate it. Turn the dough out onto a lightly floured surface and form into a ball. Let it rest for 5 minutes on the work surface before you shape it.

7. Depending on the shape of your slow cooker dish, shape the dough to an oval or round. Line the base and sides of the slow cooker dish with baking parchment, and place the dough in the center.

8. Cover the dish with the lid and switch the cooker on to a warm setting. Leave the bread to rise for 1 hour. If your machine doesn't have a warm setting, leave the covered dish in a warm place until doubled in size.

9. When ready to cook, switch the cooker to high and cook for 3½ to 4 hours, until risen and the top of the bread feels firm and springs back when lightly pressed. If your cooker produces a lot of moisture on the inside of the lid, lay a loose, crumpled sheet of baking parchment over the loaf after 1 hour of cooking, and quickly replace the lid. This will help prevent any drips of water falling onto the loaf and making the crust soggy.

10. Transfer the bread to a wire rack to cool. For a brown crust, place the hot loaf under a preheated hot grill for a few seconds to brown, then transfer to a wire rack to cool completely.

Soda Bread

This is an easy recipe to adapt to make a whole wheat version or use ordinary all-purpose white plain flour for a classic soda bread. Add 3 oz. (75g) of any chopped dried fruit for a sweeter loaf.

Makes: one 1 lb. 9 oz. (725g), 8" (20cm) round loaf
Preparation Time: 15 minutes
Cooking Time: 45 minutes

Ingredients

- 12 oz. (350g) white spelt flour, plus extra for dusting
- 1 tsp. salt
- 1 tsp. baking soda
- 4 oz. (115g) whole wheat spelt flour
- 2 tsp. maple syrup
- 1 Tbsp. sunflower oil
- 10 fl. oz. (300mL) dairy or plant buttermilk (page 154)

Anyone with a recognized wheat or gluten allergy should avoid spelt flour as well as other wheat products.

Directions

1. Preheat the oven to 400°F (200°C/180°C fan oven). Sieve the white flour with the salt and soda into a bowl and stir in the whole wheat flour.

2. Make a well in the center and add the syrup and oil. Gradually pour in the buttermilk in the center of the well and gently mix using a wooden spoon to make a softish mixture.

3. Turn the mixture on to a lightly floured work surface and work it gently to tidy up the edges and neaten it.

4. Carefully transfer the mixture to a lightly floured baking tray and press it down to make a 6" (15cm) diameter, approx. 2" (5cm) thick round. Using a lame or small sharp knife, cut a deep cross in the top, right to the edges. Dust with flour and bake in the center of the oven for 45 minutes, until risen, golden, and hollow sounding when tapped underneath. Transfer to a wire rack to cool. Best eaten on the same day as baking.

Buttermilk

Available in low-fat and full-fat varieties. Choose whichever you prefer for this recipe or for the Cornbread, Banana Nut Bread, and Easy Cinnamon Bread.

To make your own buttermilk:

1. Mix 4 tsp. fresh lemon juice into 10 fl. oz. (300mL) dairy or plant milk.

2. Leave at room temperature for 15 minutes, until it thickens, then cover and chill for up to 2 days. Stir before using.

Easy Cinnamon Bread

Half cake, half bread, this sweetly spiced, nonyeasted loaf freezes well, and the mixture can also be easily made gluten free.

Makes: one 1 lb. 9½ oz. (725g) loaf

Preparation Time: 15 minutes

Cooking Time: 1 hour

Ingredients

- 4 oz. (115g) lightly salted dairy or plant butter, softened
- 7 oz. (200g) superfine sugar
- 1 medium egg or vegan egg (page 34)
- 7 fl. oz. (200mL) dairy or plant buttermilk (page 154)
- 8 oz. (225g) all-purpose flour or gluten-free bread flour
- ½ tsp. baking soda
- 1½ tsp. ground cinnamon

Directions

1. Preheat the oven to 350°F (180°C/160°C fan oven). Grease and line a 2lb (900g) loaf pan. Put the butter and 5 oz. (150g) sugar in a bowl. Add the egg or vegan egg, and beat until creamy and well blended.

2. Stir in the milk and sift the flour and baking soda on top. Mix to form a thick batter. In a separate bowl, mix the remaining sugar with the cinnamon.

3. Spoon half the batter into the prepared pan and sprinkle half the cinnamon sugar evenly on top. Use a skewer or toothpick to swirl the sugar into the batter, then spoon over the remaining cake batter, sprinkle with the remaining cinnamon sugar, and repeat the swirling.

4. Smooth the top and bake for about 1 hour until risen and a skewer inserted into the center comes out clean. Leave to cool for 20 minutes before removing from the pan and cooling on a wire rack.

Cornbread

Perfect for mopping up soups and stews, this nonyeasted bread can be quickly made and baked. Leave out the sweetcorn kernels if preferred. For a smoky flavor, add two teaspoons of smoked paprika. It's easy to make gluten free as well.

Makes: one 1 lb. 12 oz. (800g), 6" (15cm) diameter loaf
Preparation Time: 15 minutes
Cooking Time: 1 hour

Ingredients

- 5 oz. (150g) all-purpose flour or gluten-free bread flour
- 5 oz. (150g) masa harina (fine cornmeal)
- 1 tsp. baking soda
- 1 tsp. baking powder
- ½ tsp. salt

- 1 Tbsp. superfine sugar
- 2 medium eggs, beaten or vegan egg (page 34)
- 5 tsp. corn oil
- 4 oz. (115g) cooked sweetcorn
- 10 fl. oz. (300mL) dairy or plant buttermilk (page 154)

Directions

1. Preheat the oven to 350°F (180°C/160°C fan oven). Grease and line a 7" (18cm) diameter, 3" (7.5cm) deep round pan.

2. Sieve the flour, cornmeal, baking soda, baking powder, salt, and sugar in a bowl and make a well in the center. Add the eggs or vegan egg, oil, and sweetcorn. Mix using a wooden spoon.

3. Gradually mix in the buttermilk to make a smooth, thick batter. Transfer to the prepared pan and bake in the center of the oven for about 1 hour until golden and risen, and until a skewer inserted into the center comes out clean. Turn on to a wire rack to cool. Best served warm, cut into thick slices.

Banana Nut Bread

This nonyeasted loaf has become a much-loved bake over the years and is easy to make gluten free. It contains chopped walnuts, but these can easily be left out if preferred or replaced with chocolate chips for extra indulgence.

Makes: one 1 lb. 7 oz. (650g) loaf
Preparation Time: 10 minutes
Cooking Time: 55 minutes

Ingredients

- 6 oz. (175g) cake flour or gluten-free bread flour
- 4½ oz. (125g) superfine sugar
- ½ tsp. baking powder
- ½ tsp. baking soda
- 3 oz. (75g) unsalted dairy or plant butter, softened
- 5 oz. (150g) very ripe banana (approx. 2 ripe, medium bananas), mashed
- 4 Tbsp. (60mL) dairy or plant buttermilk (page 154)
- 1 medium egg or vegan egg (page 34)
- 2 oz. (50g) walnuts, chopped

Directions

1. Preheat the oven to 350°F (180°C/160°C fan oven). Grease and line a 2lb (900g) loaf pan. Sieve the flour, sugar, baking powder, and baking soda into a bowl.

2. Make a well in the center of the dry ingredients and add the butter, banana, and buttermilk. Mix until all the flour is coated then beat well for 2 minutes.

3. Add the egg or vegan egg, and beat well for a further 2 minutes. Stir in the walnuts and transfer the mixture to the prepared pan. Smooth the top and bake for about 55 minutes, until risen and a skewer inserted into the center comes out clean. Leave to cool for 10 minutes before removing from the pan and cooling on a wire rack.

Corn Tortillas

There is quite an art to make perfectly round tortillas, and special presses are available to do the job for you. Rolling thinly by hand will make perfectly acceptable tortillas, and once you are well practiced, you will be able to make them neater and rounder.

Makes: six 7" (18cm) diameter, 2 oz. (50g) tortillas
Preparation Time: 30 minutes
Cooking Time: 24 minutes

Ingredients

- 4½ oz. (125g) all-purpose flour
- 4½ oz. (125g) masa harina (fine cornmeal)
- ½ tsp. salt
- 2 Tbsp. (30mL) corn oil
- 4 fl. oz. (115mL) lukewarm water

Directions

1. Sieve the flours into a large mixing bowl and stir in the salt. Make a well in the center and add the oil. Gradually pour and mix in the water using a wooden spoon, carefully stirring in the dry ingredients from the outside of the bowl to form a softish, ball-like mixture in the center of the bowl.

2. Turn on to a lightly floured surface and knead gently for 1–2 minutes to make a soft, smooth ball of dough. Cover with a clean tea towel or cheesecloth (muslin). Leave to rest on the surface for 15 minutes.

3. Divide the dough into 6 equal pieces and form each into a ball.

4. Dust the work surface with a little flour and roll one ball at a time, as thinly as possible, turning and shaping the dough to prevent it sticking and to keep it as round as possible, until it measures 7" (18cm), about $1/12$" (2mm) thick.

5. Heat a large frying pan over a high heat for 1 minute. Reduce the heat to medium and cook the tortillas one at a time for 1–2 minutes, until bubbles appear on the surface, then flip over and cook for a further 1–2 minutes, until lightly golden and toasted. Wrap them in cheesecloth (muslin) to keep them soft and warm while you cook all the dough. Best served warm.

Note

Leave to cool, and wrap well for storing up to two days. Or wrap and freeze for up to six months. To reheat, simply heat gently in a hot frying pan for a few seconds on each side.

Variation

Use all wheat flour if preferred and adjust amount of water as necessary.

Gluten-Free Variation

1. Replace the wheat flour with gluten-free bread flour (or use an all-purpose gluten-free flour blend and add xanthan gum) and mix with the corn flour, oil and about 2 Tbsp. (30mL) extra water.

2. Mix the ingredients until they come together into a workable, smooth dough; divide into 6 and roll as above.

3. The dough will be more challenging to roll thinly and does tear easily. Use a palette knife to slide under the rolled-out dough to help turn it on the worktop and transfer to the frying pan. Cook and store in the same way.

Photo Credits

All Photos © Stuart MacGregor (unless listed in the Shutterstock images below)

All images from Shutterstock.com:
Page 2: mihalec. **Page 4:** Maksym Fesenko. **Pages 8–9:** Drazen Zigic. **Page 10:** Sarnia (top right); Novikov Aleksey (bottom). **Page 11:** Omfotovideocontent (top); Elena_Alex_Ferns (bottom right). **Page 12:** Michalakis Ppalis (top); jsp (bottom right). **Page 13:** PosiNote (top right); David Fadul (bottom left). **Page 14:** Leon Rafael (top left); Michalakis Ppalis (bottom). **Page 15:** Fotosanti76. **Page 16:** Roman Zaiets (top right); Gamzova Olga (bottom left). **Page 17:** AGCuesta (top right); Africa Studio (bottom left). **Page 20:** PhotoFires (top); Roman023_Photography (bottom right). **Page 21:** 279photoStudio. **Page 22:** Andrii Horulko (top right); TimeLineArtist (bottom left). **Page 27:** Moving Moment. **Page 28:** Daisy Daisy. **Page 33:** msheldrake. **Page 43:** Maksym Fesenko. **Page 44:** Africa Studio (top); Casezy idea (bottom right). **Page 45:** Anze Furlan (top); BBPPHOTO (bottom left). **Page 49:** Sebastian_Photography. **Pages 66–67:** Paul Cowan.**Page 68:** Tei Sinthip. **Page 70:** Petar Ivanove Ishmiriev. **Page 72:** rsooll. **Page 73:** Trending Now. **Page 74:** sophiecat. **Page 75:** eleonimages (top right); ANUCHA PONGPATIMETH (bottom left). **Page 81:** pink.mousy (wheat background.) **Page 84:** pink.mousy (wheat background.) **Page 87:** Nataly Studio. **Page 90:** pink.mousy (wheat background.) **Page 93:** bergamont. **Page 96:** pink.mousy (wheat background.) **Page 105:** Oksana Mizina. **Page 108:** pink.mousy (wheat background.) **Page 111:** Nataly Studio. **Page 112:** pink.mousy (wheat background.) **Page 122:** Tiger Images. Page 123: VITTO-STUDIO. **Page 126:** pink.mousy (wheat background.) **Page 128:** New Africa. **Page 129:** pink.mousy (wheat background .) **Page 132:** pink.mousy (wheat background.) **Page 135:** Christian Jung. **Page 138:** pink.mousy (wheat background.) **Page 141:** Princess_Anmitsu. **Page 144:** pink.mousy (wheat background.) **Page 150:** pink.mousy (wheat background.) **Page 153:** BestPix. **Page 162:** Galayko Sergey.

Bibliography

Davidson, Alan. *The Oxford Companion of Food*. Oxford: Oxford University Press, 1999.
Giagnocavo, Carole Ruth and Mennonite Central. *Amish Community Cookbook*. Mount Joy: Fox Chapel Publishing, 2020.
Hadjiandreou, Emmanuel. *How to Make Bread*. London: Ryland Peters & Small, 2011.
Hawkins, Kathryn. *Bread!*. London: New Holland, 2006.
Hawkins, Kathryn. *Self-Sufficiency: Breadmaking*. Lincolnshire: IMM Lifestyle Books, 2016.
McGee, Harold. *On Food and Cooking*. London: Hodder and Stoughton, 2004.
Montagné, Prosper. *Larousse Gastronomique*. 2nd English ed. Edited by Jenifer Harvey Lang. New York: Crown Publishers, 1988.
Treuille, Eric and Ursula Ferrigno. *Bread*. London: Dorling Kindersley, 1998.

Index

Index

About the Author

Kathryn Hawkins is an experienced recipe and food writer. She has a passion for baking and has authored more than 20 books, including *Bread!; Chocolate!; Crepes, Waffles and Pancakes!;* and *Comfort Pie.* Aside from her writing, Kathryn is a food stylist and home economist. She was cookery editor at *Woman's Own* magazine and has worked on a wide range of consumer publications. She also prepares food for photography used in advertising, packaging, television, and online.

Acknowledgments

I'd like to thank photographer Stuart MacGregor for his dedication and patience throughout the time it took to photograph the recipes for this book and for his fine attention to detail, which has given this book such superior images. I'd also like to thank the team at Fox Chapel for giving me the opportunity to revise this book and for all the help and support they have offered throughout the project.